Facilitating an Everyday Life

INDEPENDENT FACILITATION AND WHAT REALLY MATTERS IN A NEW STORY

John Lord
Barbara Leavitt
Charlotte Dingwall

INCLUSION

Library and Archives Canada Cataloguing in Publication

Lord, John, 1943-
    Facilitating an everyday life : independent facilitation and what really matters in a new story / John Lord, Barbara Leavitt, Charlotte Dingwall.

Includes bibliographical references.
ISBN 978-1-895418-73-6

    1. People with disabilities--Services for. 2. Counselor and client.
I. Leavitt, Barbara, 1962- II. Dingwall, Charlotte, 1960- III. Title.

HV1568.L67 2012   362.4'0486   C2012-902314-0

Book Cover Painting - Sarah Lord

Published by Inclusion Press
Copyright © 2012 Inclusion Press

Printed in Canada by Couto Printing & Publishing
Printed on stock containing post consumer recycled content

INCLUSION PRESS

47 Indian Trail   tel. 416.658.5363   inclusionpress@inclusion.com
Toronto, ON M6R 1Z8   fax. 416.658.5067   inclusion.com

inclusion.com   BOOKS • WORKSHOPS • MEDIA • RESOURCES

Facilitating an Everyday Life

Independent Facilitation
and What Really Matters in a New Story

Life… is in the living, the tissue
of every day and hour.

Stephen Leacock

Introduction

I t was a warm summer day when we first got together to begin to make this book a reality. But the truth is that it had been a growing idea for many years as we each have journeyed through various roles in our communities.

We have been part of an increasing number of individuals who believe that people, communities, and services need a New Story. Many of the systems created to help simply do not provide the necessary supports for people who have been labelled or who are vulnerable because of disability, chronic illness, poverty, or aging to live an everyday life. This New Story idea was originally explored in-depth in the book by John Lord and Peggy Hutchison, *Pathways to Inclusion: Building a New Story with People and Communities.*

In a New Story, there are many important levers for change, and independent facilitation is one of the most important. And this is where we began on that warm summer day.

What compelled us to focus on independent facilitation was our experience with the difference it makes in people's lives. We get excited talking about the depth and range of independent facilitation. As an independent facilitator there is the freedom to listen and to respond without traditional constraints. There is the satisfaction of being dedicated to a single person and how they want their life to unfold. And there is the beauty of building a relationship with someone while having few predetermined assumptions about possibilities.

We know we are on the right path: research has shown over and over that independent facilitation leads to positive community experiences for people.

Independent facilitation is an emerging craft. Facilitators in the New Story believe that community is always the answer. We reject approaches that do not lead people to relationships in their community. And while independent facilitation frequently touches the service system to access supports for a person, it is independent of agendas, expectations, and accountabilities of service systems.

This book is for people like us, people who want to make a difference, who want to feel free to be dedicated to a person, who want to use an effective process that is a change-maker. Becoming skilled at independent facilitation is often more about the ordinariness than the big flashes — a homeless man choosing (finally!) to have a hot lunch every day at the soup kitchen, but not yet (if ever) choosing to leave the streets. This book is for people who are not always looking for a fairy tale ending, but who see the beauty in helping people build an everyday life, and in doing so sometimes see big change.

As facilitators, we bring our life experience to this work. John is a researcher who initially learned the craft over many years of working on community research projects, where collaboration with vulnerable citizens was central to the work. As a father of a daughter with a disability, he also has direct experience with the challenges and joys of his daughter living an everyday life. He has played a leadership role in developing New Story ideas through his previous publications.

Barbara has worked as an independent facilitator in several areas of Ontario, as well as working in various roles in the service system. She also has personal experience in navigating systems and community with someone she loves who lives with autism. Barbara now works in the public health field where her work with social determinants of health constantly informs her facilitation.

Charlotte is a facilitator and has been for many years, both in a community organization and independently. She has been involved with an Ontario provincial initiative designed to enhance independent facilitation. Charlotte has intimate understanding of the power of relationships to effect change in someone's life. She is currently involved in building an independent facilitation and planning organization.

We all now work as trainers of facilitators and find we are always learning in this process of teaching! Our work with the Facilitation Leadership Group has engaged us with several communities in Canada and the U.K. who are working to implement a New Story. We find that people are hungry for conversation and reflection about facilitation and ways to include people in everyday life.

As facilitators we are both patient and impatient. We always walk with people at their pace, encouraging, questioning, and supporting growth and change. There is a deliberate patience to this work and a commitment to staying with people as they build their lives in their communities. We also notice injustice and the numerous barriers faced by people who need support to participate in community life. We are impatient with the slow pace of change in our communities and service systems, and work with others to create positive change.

Although we are experienced facilitators, the process of creating this book has deepened our insights into our own facilitation. And this is how it should be for facilitators: standing still to reflect in order to move ahead and hone our craft.

The book is structured in a linear way by necessity, but each chapter is intertwined with all others. How can you talk about relationships without talking about community! The chapters move from the craft of facilitation and the values, knowledge, and skills needed by facilitators, to ways the craft is used to support self-determination, relationships, community connections, planning, and building safeguards.

We believe this book is needed now, as many communities and service systems are undergoing significant changes in philosophy and approach. We expect that some readers are already embracing the values and principles of a New Story, while other readers will be facilitators in search of a meaningful framework. Still others may not have thought of themselves as facilitators, but in reality are doing a lot of informal facilitation. This book will contribute to practical, knowledge-based approaches to facilitation. You may be searching for ideas on how to build an everyday life. Or you may be a facilitator, a family member, a member of someone's network or support circle, a leader in the non-profit sector, an outreach worker, a neighbourhood leader, a community developer, a support co-ordinator, a social service worker, or a manager in service systems. Whatever your role, this book will bring to light the important aspects of facilitation.

We have a vision of community; we see communities and services changing to include all citizens in every aspect of community life. Facilitation that is independent plays a key role in this vision of abundant communities. We believe there is a growing number of facilitators and facilitators-to-be who share this vision. We invite you to find yourselves in these pages and reflect on how you can bring a New Story to your community through facilitation.

The beauty of independent facilitation

Independent facilitation puts belief and hope in community because that is where relationships and safeguards play out for all of us.

Independent facilitation frees facilitators to be dedicated to the person they are engaged with and are independent of biases from other pressures such as service systems and funding bodies.

Independent facilitation builds resilience and capacity in individuals, families, and communities.

Independent facilitation flourishes when it is embedded in community, in facilitator networks, and is supported by local action and government policy.

Principles that guide independent facilitation

Self-Determination

1. The power of decision-making about the person's life rests with the person and others whom he/she chooses.
2. People's strengths, as well as what they imagine for their future, guide how they build an everyday life.

Community

3. Community is the first resort in building a good life.
4. Relationships and networks of people are intentionally developed.

Capacity Building

5. Independent facilitation leverages strengths in individuals and groups to mobilize people to act in new ways.
6. Funding for supports and services is individualized and portable.

Chapter One

Claiming an Everyday Life

Most of us take the experiences of an everyday life for granted. We have a place to call home, we go to work. Life is busy. We are involved with family and friends. Neighbours may ask for a favour. The phone rings regularly, email and text messages await our replies. We volunteer for a local organization. We read the local newspaper and very often know some of the people in the stories or photos (or know someone who would). We experience the highs and lows of life and have people to share them with. We find meaning in our daily activities and personal connections.

At the same time, others in our communities struggle to experience this kind of everyday life. People with disabilities are unemployed at two to three times the rate of non-disabled citizens and many are segregated in group homes, boarding houses, and day programs. It is not unusual for people with mental health issues to feel lonely and isolated and to experience fragmented, limited supports. Older persons, especially those who are frail, often experience medicalized lives with few connections to the wider community. And far too many people are homeless, unable to find the energy or the resources to have a roof over their heads. They live well below the poverty line and experience poor health status. For too many of our fellow citizens, claiming an everyday life is not easy.[1]

> *As we think about what an everyday life means, we understand that it includes all the little things that add up to make life meaningful.*

As we think about what an everyday life means, we understand that it includes all the little things that add up to make life meaningful. In a rich life, energy and expectations change as life changes and unfolds. Hopes and dreams change as we have new experiences. Yet, too many people in our communities experience low expectations in ways that limit a fulfilling life.

In the stories that follow, we might initially think that each person is experiencing a reasonable life. But, as we reflect on the meaning of an everyday life, we realize that these narratives are just the beginning, the entryway to begin a new path to everyday life. Sometimes the challenges involved in striving for an everyday life seem overwhelming, yet we can also see so much potential in each situation.

- When Joe Nelson finally left the psychiatric hospital, he found himself living in a room at a boarding house. Several years later, he continues to live in that same room; he has few friends, and remains disconnected from his family. A case manager looks in on Joe once a month. Joe is an avid reader and gets books from the local library every week, but would like to do much more with his life.

- When Liz Stewart was 25 years old, a group home space opened for her. Her parents were delighted to accept this 'placement', because this was how they assumed people with developmental disabilities lived. Liz has lived in that group home for twenty years and continues to attend a sheltered workshop with the same people year after year. Liz has occasionally had a job in the community, but whenever it falters, she returns to the workshop. When the phone rings it is never for her and she often says she'd like to be as busy as the staff.

- When Bart Reynolds experienced a spinal cord injury because of a swimming accident, he spent months in rehabilitation. When he was ready to return home, he went to live with his parents. He is anxious to live on his own again, but requires help to plan how that can happen. Prior to his accident, Bart was a school teacher. He would love to work with children again, but is frustrated because he is not sure where to turn.

- When Mary Robert lost her husband, it left a huge hole in her heart and in her social life. With Parkinson's disease impacting her mobility, Mary can no longer drive or use the computer. Although she receives home care support three times a week, Mary does not have any family or friends in the area to provide support and companionship. Mary had always done everything with her husband and now finds herself isolated. She has a strong desire to meet old friends and to be re-engaged in community life.

A Compelling Need for Change

These stories are all too familiar. They are also painful because it is easy to imagine how things turn out—that people will continue to live as they do now. It is assumed they cannot change and don't have the capacity to change. Frustration is also central in these stories. Yet we can also see vast untapped potential in each person's story that could be developed with appropriate support and resources. We know that enabling people to claim an everyday life will require new ways of thinking.

We know that enabling people to claim an everyday life will require new ways of thinking.

Unfortunately, most formal human services often fail to meet the personal needs and social expectations of citizens. Conventional service systems lack flexibility and seldom bring social innovation to their work. Traditionally, these service systems were created on the belief that power is best held by institutions, organizations, and professionals. At the same time, however, many of us are learning about the limits of systems and professionalization.

In conventional human services, large organizations deliver services to the people who are 'clients'. Over time, many of these organizations have come to be all things for the person. It is not unusual to find the service provider offering a myriad of personal supports, advocacy, outreach, education, housing, family support, and even counselling. When power is invested in the service provider, users are typically tied to that organization for all their supports. In this way, formal service systems tend to 'manage' the lives of people they support. These kinds of service systems have not proven to be very successful when it comes to people building good lives in the community. Despite much rhetoric to the contrary, few large organizations have been able to transform themselves.

Over the years, researchers and people using services have identified many limitations of conventional service systems. Recently, much research has highlighted the need for change which would create more individualized supports and inclusive communities.

There is growing support for new ideas that move us away from what has been called an old story.

There is growing support for new ideas that move us away from what has been called an old story. Fortunately, work over the last twenty years has identified possibilities and directions for a more positive future.

The Emergence of a New Story

Some leaders have called for a New Story to replace the old story of compliance and isolation.[2] John Lord and Peggy Hutchison, in their influential book, *Pathways to Inclusion*, identify this New Story thinking by looking at many innovative projects across Canada. The essence of this New Story is new ways of working with individuals and communities that enable people to pursue their strengths and what they imagine for a better life.

> *The essence of a New Story is new ways of working with individuals and communities that enable people to pursue their dreams and gifts in meaningful ways.*

The New Story describes a paradigm shift toward participation in community life, adequate resources and supports, and improved health and well being. It is a shift towards people living everyday lives, which leads to better outcomes for people.[3]

We have to change the way we think.

> *We have to move to a philosophy and culture rooted in person capacity, valuing people for their contribution, and to an asset-based and closer-to-community approach. This means changing our thinking so we are providing support that will enable individuals to contribute to their community based on their assets rather than providing services based on their deficiencies.[4]*

Several factors have influenced the recognition of the power of a New Story:

- *The desire of citizens who experience vulnerability themselves to have their voices heard.* Since the 1980s, people with disabilities have been raising their voices and demanding more rights and participation. More and more organizations are recognizing the need to involve people who use their service in the process of decision-making. Recently, for example, people with disabilities from around the world were instrumental in working with the United Nations in developing a Convention on the Rights of Persons with Disabilities.

- *The growth of person-directed thinking.* Although person-centred planning has been used for the last two decades, it is only recently that several social movements have embraced genuine person-directed thinking. This means that individuals and families determine the supports and relationships they require in their lives.

- *The recognition of community as crucial for citizenship and full participation.* The growth of a community focus means that community connections are seen as vital to building an everyday life. Participation in community takes many forms and includes families, neighbourhoods, and social groups that make up community life.

- *The understanding of the power of relationships as a key to health and well-being.* Research shows that among the determinants of health, relationships and social support are some of the most important. People who have rich, meaningful relationships are more likely to be healthy than people who are isolated and lonely.

- *The growing understanding that facilitation and collaboration are key roles in the New Story.* More and more success stories of community change identify collaboration as a key element of the change. When people and groups work together with a common vision, the impact on communities can be potent.

Key Components of the New Story

There are several functions of the New Story that help people to live everyday lives in the community. The functions are both separate and interdependent. They all work together to ensure that people have more control over the resources, including the design of services intended to support them. This is a marked contrast with conventional service systems, where all functions are organized within one service structure.

- Funding is flexible and individualized, so that people have control over the customized supports they require. Direct, individualized funding has been shown to enable positive outcomes for people.

- *Independent facilitation*, separate from direct service provision, creates facilitation for individuals and families. Facilitators assist people to build an everyday life.

It is important that facilitation in the New Story be independent from service provision so that individuals and families can consider what they really want and need, not just what is available.

Why Facilitation Needs to be Independent

1. Independent planning and facilitation is a process guided by certain values and principles, notably the values of self-determination, autonomy, citizenship, and using the community "as the first resort and resource" for finding the needed supports for individuals. It enables a focus on a specific mission.

2. Because of the broader mandate of agencies involved in direct supports, there are resource trade-off questions that arise, especially for those with complex needs. If supported decision making, planning, and community building for an individual are complicated and time-consuming, it is likely that corners will be cut in order to devote scarce resources elsewhere in the organization. For instance, if a person who does not speak is somewhere safe and secure and does not register complaints for some unacceptable behaviour, it's easy to conclude the result is satisfactory and turn to other business. A focus on the goals and needs would likely reveal that this person has little control over important decisions, few relationships outside family and service workers, and little opportunity to contribute to and benefit from the life of the community.

3. A significant body of empirical research from other jurisdictions shows that independent facilitation results in different outcomes from other planning and facilitation services. The advantages are especially evident in those studies which are careful to measure outcomes in terms of quality of life indicators. These try to measure such things as degree of self-determination, involvement in the community, involvement in meaningful and reciprocal relationships, and satisfaction with one's circumstances, not merely "quality and quantity of service provided."

4. Experience from facilitators who have worked in both independent and agency-based settings suggest that when working in an agency, whatever "firewalls" are supposed to be in place, the practice of looking to the community as a first resource and resort cannot be maintained. Instead, whether in times of crisis or as a part of a plan, the first resort for support and services is the employer agency or another agency. Few of us in any field can avoid having the question of who is signing our pay cheques influence our behaviour, so it's rather a lot to expect facilitators to be different.

David DeVidi
The I in Independent Planning and Facilitation
2008, Modeling Community Change and Innovation Project

- *Autonomous family networks and peer self-help groups* that support, educate, and advocate. These networks and groups provide an important place for families and people who require support to connect and learn from each other.

- *Responsive service providers* who are driven by sound values and principles in the way they support people to live their lives. Service providers in the New Story embrace the other functions and provide person-centred supports and services.

Independent Facilitation is Powerful

One of the most exciting aspects of the New Story is the role of independent facilitation. Independent facilitation refers to the idea that citizens who are excluded or vulnerable can benefit from someone (a facilitator) walking with them in their journey to claim an everyday life.

Independent facilitation refers to the idea that citizens who are excluded or vulnerable can benefit from someone (a facilitator) walking with them in their journey to claim an everyday life.

Independent facilitation builds resilience and capacity in a person, family, and community. The facilitator is an ally who supports people to develop a vision and direction for their future and responds directly to a person's strengths and dreams. Independent facilitation does this by building strong relationships and networks, creating a good person-directed planning process, and connecting others in the wider community. Ultimately, independent facilitation enables people to belong in community and experience an everyday life in families, in neighbourhoods, in self-help networks, and always in relationships.

It is important that facilitation in the New Story be independent from service provision so that individuals and families can consider what they really want and need, not just what is available.

The facilitator can sometimes be like a coach, providing support and encouragement, and assisting a team of people to work together to achieve positive results.

Think about the four people mentioned earlier. Consider how Joe, Liz, Bart, and Mary might be experiencing a different life if they had someone

> 66 *Being independent of service provision means I can give my full attention to the person and their hopes and dreams. People are often surprised that I don't provide a menu of options, but once they realize that they are in charge of the directions we will pursue, it is very empowering. As facilitators, we are not in the business of fixing, but rather walking with people in their journey.* 99

to assist them to change their environment and to imagine a better everyday life!

Facilitation has a long history in social change. Paulo Freire's ground-breaking work with poor and oppressed people in Latin America helped activists in the 1970s to see the power of dialogue and genuine, critical questions.[5] Although facilitation is now used in many areas, including business, it had its roots in democratic, bottom-up change. Facilitators engage people in conversation, ask meaningful questions, and help people to analyze their situation and recognize the possibilities in front of them.

Facilitation comes from the French word 'facile' and the Latin 'facilis': easy to do and meaning 'to make easy'. In Greek, facilitation means to 'draw out'. When done well, facilitation helps people define and live a good life. But for many people facing challenges who have little opportunity or experience with making decisions, this is not a simple matter.

Facilitation involves the use of effective processes, tailored to individual circumstances, and helps people resolve issues through genuine dialogue, effective planning, useful problem-solving and thoughtful action. Although this may appear simple to those participating, the reality is that facilitation is a craft that is honed over time.

Despite the growing and widespread appeal of independent facilitation, it has only recently been seen as a vital approach for citizens who may require support to claim an everyday life and be fully included in community.

- Facilitators support people to use their voices in whatever ways they express themselves. As importantly, they help everyone around the person respect that voice.

- Facilitators guide person-directed processes, like planning.

- Facilitators have a significant role in supporting people to build the community connections that can lead to a full, everyday life.

- The facilitator role in human services grows out of the recognition that individuals and families benefit from guidance and advice as they learn to navigate community and services.

- Facilitators know that belonging is an important part of our humanity and look to community first for possibilities.

The facilitator is enabling people and their networks of family and friends to build a life in community that includes participation and contribution. The facilitator is aware of the entire process, but recognizes that others must do much of the work for the process to be successful. Facilitation is very mindful work. When we work in the New Story, we must engage hearts and minds to be effective.[6] We can sometimes be like a coach, providing support and encouragement, and assisting a team of people to work together to achieve positive results.

The facilitator supports the power that lies within the person and others in the person's life, by providing information, guidance, community connections, and network development opportunities.

It is not surprising that independent facilitation is emerging as a key function of new paradigms designed to support citizens who have been excluded from community life. After thirty years of community-based services, anomalies abound in conventional systems. Research on paradigm shifts shows that anomalies are the first stage of paradigm change.

There are three main anomalies that impact people's desire for change:

- People want control of their lives, but are often 'stuck' in systems that give them little control over both the big and little things in their lives.

- People imagine a better life and have many strengths, but are given little support to pursue them.

- People want to belong in community, but have little opportunity or support to build meaningful relationships with a range of people in their communities.

Independent facilitation is a key lever for change because it addresses these three persistent anomalies. Unlike most service systems, facilitators start not just with the person, but also with his or her environment. They look for strengths and

Facilitators start, not just with the person, but also with their environment.

Facilitators in the New Story stay focused on what an everyday life looks like and keep the picture of that everyday life in the forefront.

capacities, and enable people to become part of community life.

Facilitators who are independent of service systems can stand with people, look at their environment, and do whatever it takes to assist that person and their networks. We can do this most effectively when we are unencumbered by service system rules, policies and regulations. We support the power that lies within a person and others in the person's life, by providing information, guidance, community connections, and network development opportunities. As facilitators in the New Story, we stay focused on what an everyday life looks like and keep the picture of that everyday life in the forefront.

Types of Facilitation

Facilitation can be either formal or informal. Formal facilitation happens when someone has the prime responsibility to facilitate for a person and their network of family and friends, a family, or a group.

In much of the western world, *formal facilitation* is an emerging part of new paradigm or New Story initiatives. In many of these cases, facilitators work for an independent facilitation organization that provides ongoing facilitation for individuals and families. In other cases, facilitators are self-employed and are hired by an agency or a family. Sometimes facilitators are family members and may be part of a family network.

Mary's family has experienced *formal facilitation*. When Mary's son, David, was about to leave high school, a facilitator from an independent organization spent time with David and the family, facilitating conversations about what life could look like after high school. The facilitator also helped the family identify and involve other people who could be helpful to this process. The facilitator helped lead several group gatherings of people that David and Mary had identified. David is now about to leave high school and he feels confident that he has a direction and supports in place. The facilitator will stay connected with Mary, David, and his network to help them safeguard a good life in community.

Informal facilitation happens when anyone facilitates with another person or group. Informal facilitation happens in many areas of life – parenting, recreation leadership, neighbourhood association meetings, faith group gatherings, self-help groups, and support workers supporting someone to live independently and participate in community. Informal facilitation grows whenever people participate together. We have all experienced informal facilitation.

Tim uses informal facilitation in his role as a support worker. His job is to assist people in their daily lives. Essentially, he helps people carry out their wishes for how they want to live their lives. He supports and encourages, but is not a decision maker. He takes direction from the person he is working with. He asks good questions and listens carefully to be sure he is doing what the person wants.

Facilitators rely on and nurture both formal and informal facilitation to bring the New Story to people's lives.

This book explores the role of independent facilitators in the New Story. As facilitators, we understand and live the values of inclusion, and we are dedicated to being with people as needed on their life journeys. We bring everything back to the experiences of an everyday life. Is there a place to call home? Does this person want more from

> *In the reflective work of New Story facilitation, facilitators bring everything back to the experiences of an everyday life.*

life — employment, more time with family, or to make new friends? Have relationships with neighbours been developed? Does the phone ring regularly? Does the person experience the highs and lows of life and have people to share that with? Is life busy and meaningful? Has this person claimed an everyday life?

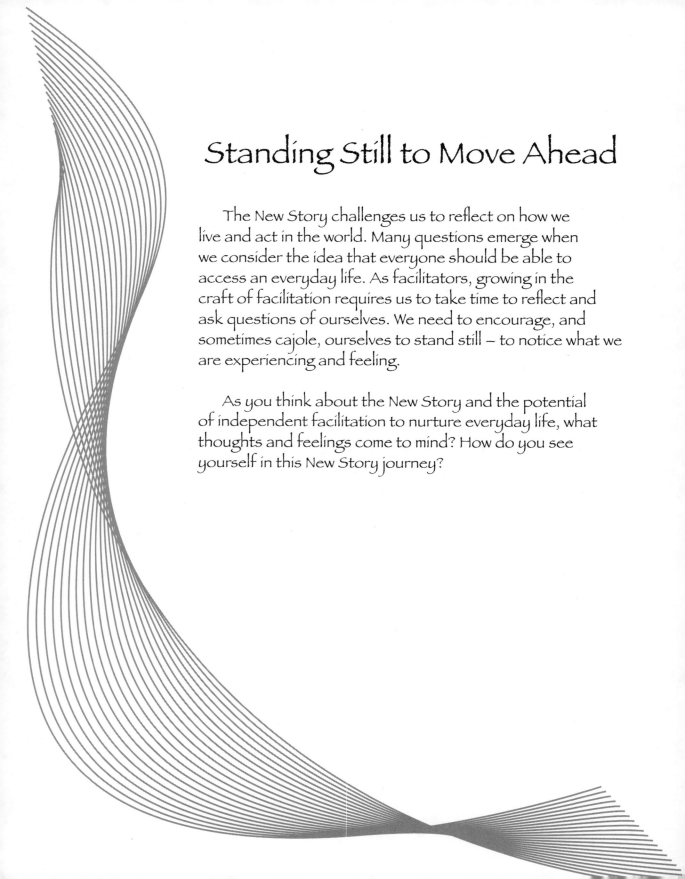

Standing Still to Move Ahead

The New Story challenges us to reflect on how we live and act in the world. Many questions emerge when we consider the idea that everyone should be able to access an everyday life. As facilitators, growing in the craft of facilitation requires us to take time to reflect and ask questions of ourselves. We need to encourage, and sometimes cajole, ourselves to stand still – to notice what we are experiencing and feeling.

As you think about the New Story and the potential of independent facilitation to nurture everyday life, what thoughts and feelings come to mind? How do you see yourself in this New Story journey?

Chapter Two

Grounding Our Work as Facilitators

Our work as facilitators is grounded in a framework that guides our efforts with individuals, families, and communities. Facilitators in the New Story bring three interactive elements to this framework: values, knowledge, and skills. When these three elements are working together, the power of independent facilitation is greatest. It enables us to keep the picture of everyday life experiences alive for people, their networks of family and friends, any service providers involved, and the wider community.

Facilitators in the New Story bring three interactive elements to this framework: values, knowledge, and skills.

The Facilitator's Framework Includes Values

Facilitators are steeped in values. We have already described how facilitation focuses on citizenship, relationships, community connections, and full participation.

These cornerstones all naturally arise from the three key values that, as the New Story has evolved in the past twenty years, have become central to our work as facilitators:

- self-determination
- community
- capacity building.

The Value of Self-Determination

Self-determination is a fundamental value in democratic societies, which are supposed to be better than other political systems at recognizing the importance of allowing citizens to control their own lives. Self-determination as a key value for facilitation reflects the view that vulnerable citizens also deserve to have their voices heard. Self-determination is based on the belief that everyone wants to have control over his or her own life. And control is a significant issue for health and well-being! The World Health Organization includes in their definition of health the degree of control that citizens have in their lives.

Facilitators support person-directed thinking and the simple idea that people should have a significant say in the direction of their own lives.

The growth of self-determination as a movement also reflects the expansion of person-directed thinking. People who require supports to live full lives in community say they often have little control over the things that matter – when to go to bed, what they eat, how their support is provided, who they live with, and where they go in the community. Facilitators support person-directed thinking and the simple idea that people should have a significant say in the direction of their own lives.

Self-determination, then, is about people being able to pursue their intentions, to be able to make informed choices, and to be a full participant in all aspects of their lives. We honour the value of self-determination in our work with individuals, families, and their networks.

The Value of Community

Community as a key value reflects the recognition of community as an important resource for citizenship and full participation, and the power of relationships as a key to health and well-being.

Community refers to those places and spaces that bring relationships to our lives.

Community refers to those places and spaces that bring relationships to our lives. We all know what it feels like to belong or to be part of community. Yet, some people are still absent from community and civic life. Whether it is a neighbourhood, a network of people, or a community organization where people gather around common interests, community is all around us. Facilitators honour the value of community and always look to community for connections and possibilities.

The Value of Capacity Building

Capacity building as a key value reflects the growing understanding that facilitation and collaboration are key roles in the New Story. Capacity building is first noticing strengths in individuals and groups and then leveraging those strengths to mobilize people to act in new ways. It is kind of like looking at something and suddenly seeing potential. Capacity building begins with a mindset that sees possibility and intentionally builds on that potential.

> *Capacity building is noticing the strengths in individuals and groups and then leveraging those strengths to mobilize people to act in new ways.*

Capacity building in the New Story is strength-based work. When facilitation is working well, individuals and their networks become more self-reliant over time. Facilitators are always finding ways to build capacity with individuals, families, networks, neighbourhoods, and the wider community.

Principles Bring Values to Life

The values of self-determination, community, and capacity building each give rise to principles that guide the day to day work of facilitators. Facilitators in the New Story base their work on these three values, which come alive with clear principles.

For those new to facilitation, it is important to return to the values and principles over and over again. For those who are more seasoned, there is benefit to reflecting more deeply on each of the principles. When we are intentional about following the principles, it gradually becomes second nature to think in terms of the principles as we confront new situations.

Facilitators use principles in their work with individuals, families, services, and communities. When facilitators are guided by principles, they see the big picture. Principles enable facilitators to stay above the fray and not be drawn into the chaos that often exists in complicated situations.

Some principles reflect the values of self-determination or community and provide guideposts for us to do deep work that advances these values. Other principles serve to build capacity of individuals, families, and communities while others contribute to social learning among people involved in the New Story. For each of these values, we outline the main principles that we use to guide our work as facilitators.

Self-Determination

1. The power of decision-making about a person's life rests with that person and others whom he/she chooses.

2. People's strengths, as well as what they imagine for their future, guide how they build an everyday life.

Community

3. Community is the first resort in building a good life.

4. Relationships and networks of people are intentionally developed.

Capacity Building

5. Independent facilitation leverages strengths in individuals and groups to mobilize people to act in new ways.

6. Funding for supports and services is individualized and portable.

Social Learning

7. Autonomous peer self-help groups and family networks educate, empower, and advocate.

8. Collaboration builds capacity and enhances problem-solving.

9. Social innovation inspires creativity, learning, and broad change.

The Facilitator's Framework Includes Knowledge

There is a growing body of knowledge that facilitators in the New Story need to understand and use in their work. Concepts such as community, strengths-based approaches, person-directed planning, social network development, group process, and community development each have a body of theory and research. For example, recent research on social networks shows that people's networks are much more influential in many areas of their lives than previously realized.

An appreciation of this kind of knowledge can steer facilitators in making evidence-based decisions in their work. We need to be knowledgeable about community resources, relationship building, current human service programs, government programs and policies, and funding approaches. Knowledge increases the possibilities and range of options that can be explored.

The Facilitator's Framework Includes Skills

Facilitation is a skilful art and science: it is a craft. The facilitator is a skilled listener, a master of good process, and has a variety of tools and techniques to draw upon as needed. When a group seems stuck, facilitators know what process to bring to that situation. When there is conflict, facilitators have options for resolution. We are able to read the needs of a group and know when to ask questions, when to slow down, and when to challenge. An experienced facilitator seems natural in their role, suggesting that with training and practice, many of the facilitation skills become intuitive and part of the style of the facilitator. Skilled facilitators help people on their journey to claim everyday life.

Standing Still to Move Ahead

Staying grounded in values, knowledge, and skills keeps us in the vision of an everyday life. As facilitators working in the New Story, we recognize that being dedicated to a person and their network is often slow, reflective work. Reflection for the facilitator is central, because it enables us to notice what is happening around us. As practitioners of the craft of facilitation, we are learning what we want to hone in our practice and what we want to leave behind. Reflection allows us to pay attention to who we are as facilitators so that we engage people in respectful ways, honouring a process that makes sense for the person. Our reflective practice shows in the way we learn to adapt to the unexpected, the ease with which we listen to troubling stories, and how over time we become comfortable with the craft of facilitation.

As you reflect on the values, knowledge, and skills, where do you feel you need the most training and practice? What will support you in your journey to become a reflective facilitator? What actions and commitments can you make that will enhance your craft?

Chapter Three

Honing the Craft of Facilitation

We have already outlined a framework that grounds our facilitation: values, knowledge, and skills. This anchors us in what is important and provides direction for the facilitator in guiding people to build more inclusive lives. As part of this framework, we need to embrace the craft of facilitation itself. A craft can be thought of as skilled work. But the craft of facilitation is more than just a box of formulaic tools. Guided by clear values and sound knowledge, we use various skills and tools to create effective processes with people.

Facilitators hone their craft through practice and reflection. At first, we will want to be very intentional about each element of the craft. Over time, the work of facilitation becomes increasingly natural and at times effortless. Deepening the craft

Facilitators hone the craft of facilitation through practice and reflection.

of facilitation is like learning to dance. At first it may feel awkward, and lack co-ordination, but with practice the dancers flow and move in time to the music. And facilitators are always committed to learning new dances!

Facilitators new to the craft need to be patient and be open to practicing in all kinds of situations. As explored previously, there are many opportunities to practice informal facilitation, in neighbourhoods, with families, and in workplaces. This practice helps confirm what facilitators probably already know; that people respond to skilled facilitation processes.

The craft of facilitation weaves together skills and knowledge through a number of identifiable stages:

- listening and noticing
- constructing meaningful conversations
- building and holding good processes
- moving to action
- documenting both process and outcomes.

Listening and Noticing

The power of listening and noticing is becoming very familiar, not just to facilitators, but to anyone who is trying to engage others. If we don't listen, how will we know someone's thoughts and feelings? If we focus too much on what we think, won't we miss another person's genuine concerns? If we are too busy, how will we notice our own perceptions? If we focus primarily on our own agenda, won't we fail to notice things in the environment that may be very significant?

> " *When people do not communicate with words, sometimes others have varying opinions about what the person is saying. My role as a facilitator is to listen deeply and encourage others to do so as well. Only then do we have the possibility of finding a genuine connection with that person.* "

As Vivek Patel said, "Listening is the highest form of self-expression." There are several elements to listening and noticing, all of which enable facilitators to be mindful and aware.

- Seek first to understand to be sure that you really know what the other person is saying. Facilitators do not jump to 'fix' problems, but take time to explore meaning and context. Context is the multi-layered environment in which people live and participate.

- Pay attention to the words and the body language. Some people may express themselves very physically, while others may use words to communicate.

- Notice when you are judging what you are hearing. Facilitators seek to understand, and find that judging often gets in the way of developing insight.

- Paraphrase what the other person says to be sure you heard it correctly. The ability to summarize conversation is a critical skill for many reasons, especially in helping to move ideas to action.

- Create space for people to feel relaxed. Slowing down the pace, building hospitality, and having guidelines for group process all help people feel relaxed and begin to notice possibilities. Building inclusive settings often requires this kind of process.

- Watch for opportunities to build capacity. Facilitators are always looking for ways to build capacity of individuals, families, and communities. We notice where we can seed and support the development of skills and knowledge in others.

Listening to the Whispers

As we become more mindful in our listening and noticing, we become attuned to things that we might not have previously noticed. People who have been labelled or rejected often have a quiet voice. We learn to listen to the whispers and to the intention in people's quiet voice. We look for strengths where others may see only deficits, and we see possibilities where others may see only problems. As we notice, we ask questions. What people and places would embrace this person who is passionate about social justice? What people and places would see the gift of this person with the big smile who does not speak with words? What people and places would value the energy of this young person who seems to always be on the move?

Facilitators learn to listen to the whispers and to the intention in people's quiet voice.

A vital role for facilitators is to act as models and to coach others to listen. When people are invited to form a social network with someone, the facilitator creates space for respectful listening. And not only do we listen to the person, we need to listen to the people who support that person. When a mother says, "I am tired," we need to listen with understanding, and to move to possible alternatives. This kind of listening and noticing means suspending judgement, being able to start

An important role for facilitators is to model and coach others to listen.

" *I want to*
honour the silence
Too often we get into
You talk - I talk
Your ideas - my ideas

I want to honour the silence
To fully listen to you
To not feel any need to
"up" your view or
win an argument

I want to honour the silence
To learn from the pauses
To reflect in my entire being
To be a thinking heart "

where people are at. Facilitators honour family norms, notice hospitality and neighbourhood happenings, and sense when relationships might blossom if nurtured.

We are always reflecting on our listening skills:

- Do I pay attention to the words and body language of people who communicate in different ways?

- Do I catch myself judging what I am hearing?

- Do I paraphrase what I heard accurately?

- Do I create space for people to feel relaxed?

- Do I watch for opportunities to build capacity in others?

Constructing Meaningful Conversations

Conversations are a central part of facilitation. Conversation is interactive communication that involves meaningful exchange of ideas, thoughts, or feelings. Good conversation takes a critical investment of time. It is too easy to rush to solutions; conversation reminds us to explore possibilities and take time to engage people in meaningful discovery of what is important.

Facilitators can use conversation in multiple ways. We typically begin our work with people who want something different in their lives. These conversations are often one-on-one and cover a range of issues that the person wants to explore.

Facilitators also use conversation with people who are coming together to assist someone to build a better life in community. Increasingly, social networks (sometimes called circles of support) are being developed to provide support and friendship to someone who can benefit from fellow citizens walking with them on their journey.

Facilitators may also gather diverse people together to work on a community issue. These conversations might begin with a small group of people who are concerned with an issue, but may expand to the broader community.

The power of conversation lies in its elegant simplicity. Yet, in our complex world, we often need to create the right pace and the right space so that unhurried conversation can occur. Paul Born from Tamarack has written a wonderful book about the power of conversation. With great

> " *People I have come to know face issues that often require that we involve a range of people. When some-one is isolated and lonely, they need more than a social worker. They need a network of caring people. This work requires that we be good at convening and facilitating conversations with those people.* "

insight, *Community Conversations* shows how listening and conversation can change communities.[7] Facilitators understand that genuine conversations have a purpose and a process that invites participation and deliberation.

Constructing conversation is a key role for facilitators. Paul Born reminds us there are usually four foundations of conversations[8]: conversing, engaging, collaborating and casting a vision.

Conversing implies that facilitators are genuinely exploring meaning with other people. Because the search for common meaning can be so challenging, facilitators must be aware how certain assumptions can limit conversation.

> **Facilitators construct conversation because they understand that no one person has the answer. Facilitators are not expert oriented, they are community oriented.**

Engaging implies that convening conversations is only the beginning. Facilitators understand that when people are engaged in conversation, everyone involved can be changed! Facilitators construct conversation because they understand that for issues to be resolved, no one person has the answer. Facilitators are not expert oriented, they are community oriented.

Collaborating implies that people are working together for a common goal. Facilitators are aware that they often need to invite people from other sectors to help address an issue. People with disabilities who want better transportation can collaborate with people who share this concern, including seniors groups, transportation departments, and local businesses. Facilitators can facilitate conversations within one area, but also across sectors.

Casting a vision implies that, as people begin to deepen their community conversations, a vision for something better often emerges. Facilitators often seed and support new ideas and create space for these ideas to take root and grow. This might be with a person, a network, a neigbourhood, or a community-wide effort.

We are always checking that our conversations are meaningful:

- Do I make sure people are not hurried so that meaningful conversations can happen?
- Have I made sure all the right people are invited to the conversations?
- Do I help people get unstuck from their positions and create a dialogue?
- Do I ask good questions that can deepen conversations?

Power of Dialogue

Facilitators working within the New Story understand the limitations of debate and discussion as main tools for communication. These approaches to communication are dominated by 'positions' that people hold. When strong positions are held, with people trying to convince others that they are right, genuine conversation becomes very difficult and often divisive. For these reasons, facilitators appreciate the power of dialogue.

Asking good questions can be considered an art and a craft.

Conversation based on dialogue is emerging as a vital tool for facilitators because it can help people get unstuck from position mode. The essence of dialogue is to learn to suspend judgement and to build on the ideas and words of the previous speaker. While a discussion tends to be back and forth and somewhat linear, a dialogue tends to spiral and deepen over time. When dialogue is working, there is a collective sense of exploring questions together. Facilitators need to become good at creating space for genuine dialogue and at asking questions.

Conversation based on dialogue is emerging as a vital tool for facilitators because it can help people get unstuck from position mode.

Asking Questions

Facilitators ask questions in order to elicit knowledge, feelings, and information as well as to deepen conversation. We know that questions have implications for the kind of conversations we can facilitate. Questions have to be meaningful for participants, but also crafted in a way that enable people to move beyond limited assumptions.

Imagine someone telling a facilitator that he or she wants a group home for themselves or for a family member. Facilitators honour the perspective, but also want to engage the person in dialogue in order to understand the motivation behind their perspective. We know that people often ask for things because of traditional assumptions, limited experience, or because they do not believe anything else is possible. So, a facilitator might ask, "What is it about a group home that interests you?" This kind of question helps the person express what is really important to them — safety, for example. This also opens up all kinds of possibilities for dialogue and broadens opportunities to create a future.

Facilitators usually use informal conversational approaches to gather information, although there may be times when a more formal approach of asking questions is needed. This means that most often the questions come out naturally in conversation. As part of preparation and practice, however, the facilitator may well have written out a bit of a script for themselves and tucked it away for reference if needed.

The facilitator must be able to create questions based on the purpose they are pursuing. There is power in having a clear purpose – we need to ask clear, purposeful questions!

Asking Good Questions Means Being Aware

- Being aware of different kinds of questions can help facilitators sort out different answers. For example, people might give opinion answers to feeling or knowledge questions. Being aware of this, the facilitator can acknowledge, then follow-up to bring the person back to the original question. There are a wide range of other questions we might ask, including feeling questions, knowledge questions, and demographic questions.[9]

- For many people the tense of questions is difficult – we need to be clear if we are talking about now, the past, or some time in the future.

- Questions can be verbal, but we can also ask questions using symbols, shapes, or pictures. People with limited literacy will have much to say if given options for other ways of expressing it.

- Be aware when others answer for the person you are working with. Sometimes we will want to ask similar questions to parents and the person to see how they match up. Time with the person separate from family is essential to really get to know the individual.

- Similarly, we must be aware of who is present when asking sensitive questions. Sometimes people may not be able to answer directly or honestly if a parent or a worker is present.

- We must always be aware of cultural perspectives – certain types of questions in some cultures may not be acceptable or be considered rude.

- There are two kinds of questions that facilitators typically avoid. Dichotomous questions requiring a yes/no response do not give any depth. "How was the movie?" might be answered by "fine." Asking what the person liked about the movie might elicit a fuller response. "Why" questions are also generally avoided because they presume there is a rational reason to things. "Why did you do that?" is often answered by, "I don't know."

Building and Holding Good Processes

Facilitators construct a good process and hold it while people gain confidence and competence. Holding the process means we are responsible for being aware of everything going on, and we actively employ the necessary values, knowledge, and skills. This is mindful work, and may be invisible to observers.

In building a good process, facilitators know how important it is to have the right people involved. This is key to New Story work. If we were interested in helping someone expand his or her natural supports, we might begin by exploring who is part of that person's life now. If we were supporting a family to become more involved in their neighbourhood, we might find out who the family knows, who some of the neighbourhood leaders are, and what kind of strengths exist in that neighbourhood. These explorations will assist the person or the family to invite the right people to come together.

Building a good process involves working from the right principles. At the beginning of this book we outlined some of those key New Story principles. As facilitators become aware of what issues an individual, family, or community want to address, principles guide how we work. If we are helping someone to expand relationships, we will obviously be guided by community and relationship principles. If we are enabling someone

> **People respond best when information is provided in a timely and useful manner. Facilitators do not overload people with information, but make information sharing an extension of conversation.**

to think creatively about how to organize their formal supports, the social innovation principle will guide us. Principles ground us by providing reminders and insight about what might be useful to pursue.

Good processes are created collaboratively with people and communities. Facilitators are always checking in with the person and his or her network to be sure the process reflects their vision and directions. Building a collaborative process means identifying and working across differences as well as finding common ground. Facilitators know that gathering a diverse group together can have benefits, but such gatherings require strong facilitation and good collaborative processes.

As a collaborative process emerges, facilitators often find that they are called on to provide information, whether about community resources, programs or funding options. People respond best when information is provided in a timely and useful manner. Facilitators do not overload people with information, but make information sharing an extension of conversation.

Oftentimes, people turn to the facilitator for advice. This can be tricky. Skilled facilitators find it often makes sense to say something like, "It depends on…" and provide options for people, rather than stating a definite opinion of their own. Or, if a particular direction is emerging from all the other pieces of work, we might say, "This option does seem like a good fit with the strengths we have explored," always adding the reasons for our suggestion. The response may also be to connect people with others who have been through a similar experience, so the group can check out for themselves some possible answers to the questions they have.

A good agenda, whether for small, informal gatherings or more formal community meetings, is based on sound principles and a clear purpose.

Good processes include moving to action. Facilitators know when to encourage people to make a decision and to act on that decision. We sometimes call this 'closing the deal'. It can be difficult for people to act decisively and they may need support to do so. One thing that helps is if people see their options clearly before them as well as the implications of each option.

Good process means the facilitator is focused and attentive. Facilitators bring both narrow focus and wide focus to their facilitation of a good process. When facilitators hold the process, we are very focused and attentive. Sometimes, this means bringing a narrow focus to an idea or issue that needs resolution. At the same time, we must pay attention to the complexity of the process, such as noticing differing perspectives. With practice and experience, we learn to hold the process comfortably, with a wide focus informing us of the elements that we need to be aware of, while bringing narrow focus when it is required.

Agendas Matter (Moving to Action)

Setting an agenda grounds processes in realistic ideas and actions. A good agenda, whether for small, informal gatherings or more formal community meetings, is based on sound principles and a clear purpose. It also reflects what will be meaningful to the people who are participating in the process. Facilitators develop the agenda with the people most impacted by the agenda. If the meeting is about 'Frank finding a job,' we will collaborate with Frank in setting the agenda. If the meeting is about 'strengthening our neighbourhood,' then a few neighbourhood leaders will assist us in establishing the agenda.

As part of creating a good process, facilitators must be skilled at building an agenda.

Agenda Building Questions

1. What do we know? What are the assumptions about the process so far and the experience of participants?

2. Who are we engaging? Who is involved in the process and how have they been engaged so far?

3. What principles will anchor the agenda? What are the key principles to guide the agenda at this stage of the facilitation process?

4. What do we want people to feel, think, or act on when they leave the meeting? What process and questions will get at that?

The Actual Agenda

5. What is the purpose of this meeting or gathering?

6. Building on experience, previous action, key principles, and learning opportunities, what are 3-4 key agenda items (including hospitality, decision-making, moving to action, reflection, etc.)

Documenting the Process

Facilitators know that they have to keep track of process and progress. We document the process in several ways:

- noticing and recording aspirations and intentions of the person we are working with

- recording decisions agreed to with the person

- noticing and recording outcomes and impacts of the process.

Documentation can be informal, with the facilitator recording thoughts and feelings in their journal. Documentation can also be more formal and attached to an evaluation research process. We find it useful to have both formal and informal processes working together to maximize learning and development.

We check in with ourselves regularly about how successfully we are creating a good process.

- Do I provide information in ways that are helpful but not directive?

- Do I assist the group to make sure they stay on track with the purpose and agenda?

- Do I feel comfortable closing the deal and making sure action steps are identified?

- Do I ensure that there is a monitoring plan in place to make sure the action is happening?

- Do I document both the process and outcomes in ways that support learning and development?

Experiencing the Craft of Facilitation

Practicing the craft of facilitation weaves together listening and noticing, constructing meaningful conversations, building good processes, moving to action, and documenting. Meaningful principles underlie all of this work.

Like any craft, there is much more to it than meets the eye!

- believing that all people have wisdom and capacity
- being guided by principles
- listening deeply and being present with whatever is happening
- deciding who to invite into the process
- creating hospitality
- building trust
- developing clear purpose
- honouring self-determination
- setting an agenda
- understanding the power of relationships and building relationships (family, networks)
- exploring strengths and gifts
- imagining a future and creating a vision for that future
- turning to community first for solutions
- creating space for conversation
- gathering information
- nurturing experience
- building capacity
- planning mindfully
- connecting with community
- staying on track with purpose and agenda
- identifying action steps (who, what, where, when)
- creating possibility
- nurturing community development
- reflecting and creating ongoing learning
- connecting with other facilitators to be inspired and stay grounded in the work.

Facilitators are always building capacity with individuals, families, communities, and systems. Part of this involves constructing conversations so that people and communities can explore issues and possibilities that matter to them. As we work with others so they can resolve their own issues and set their own goals, they begin to build experience, confidence, and capacity. Ultimately, when guided by clear values and sound knowledge, facilitators practice the craft of facilitation by building good process in ways that enable people to move from ideas to the actions needed for everyday life.

Standing Still to Move Ahead

Developing the craft of facilitation takes time and intentionality. Facilitators are at risk of becoming over reliant on the same tools and processes over and over again. To counter this tendency, we expand and strengthen our craft by taking time to listen to ourselves and others. Creating good and varied processes is challenging, but it is central to the individualized nature of our work. As we stand still, we notice common elements across the processes we create. We are not facilitating to 'fix' or change a person but rather engaging and supporting others on their journeys. We are reminded again and again how important people and community are to our craft. It is 'in relationship' that we learn how to listen, how to create conversation, and how to suggest processes that might assist with the journey to an everyday life.

As you reflect on your facilitation, consider which aspects of the craft you need to be developing. What feels comfortable and even natural for you? What is most challenging for you? What actions and commitments can you make that will enhance your craft?

Chapter Four

Supporting Self-Determination

S elf-determination is a central value guiding our work as facilitators. Self-determination is about people being able to say how they want to live their everyday lives. As Bob Williams, a disability activist, says, "Self-determination is just another word for freedom."[10] Although most people do not think about the freedom that self-determination brings, adults typically make all kinds of decisions that determine their own fate. These personal choices include decisions about everyday life, such as deciding where to live, who to live with, what kind of career or employment to pursue, and what kind of community involvements to be part of.

Not everyone experiences these simple freedoms. Self-determination is the very essence of personhood. To be a person is to have rights and to be able to express those rights. We know this concept of personhood is routinely ignored. Although facilitators know better, many citizens are seen as not being capable of making decisions.

As a society, we have created systems and services that act 'in the best interest' of people. In the last century, this approach to decision-making has vested power in the hands of service systems, professionals and families. Too little attention has been paid to helping people gain the experience in decision making, confidence, and information that would allow them to have control of their own lives. We have long ignored the basic human need to have choice and control in our own lives. The assumption that people are incapable of making decisions is misguided and has led to oppression and disempowerment. When we ignore the meaning and importance of self-determination, people's lives are diminished. Facilitators understand that self-determination is not a program or part of a goal-setting exercise. Facilitators ensure that people can express self-determination in their everyday lives.

> *Facilitators understand that self-determination is not a program or part of a goal setting exercise.*

We have a long history of acting in people's best interests. And it has been, for the most part, a well-intentioned approach. But it is deeply flawed. It does not acknowledge a fundamental issue that is vital for facilitators not only to recognize, but to act on: every human being is an autonomous being.

Autonomy and What it Means for Facilitators

Autonomy, which comes from the Greek word for 'self-rule,' is the ability or capacity to make informed choices, free of coercion, based on one's own personal beliefs and values. All adults are presumed to have decision-making capacity and therefore have the right to self-determination unless decided otherwise by a legal proceeding.

Of all the roles of a facilitator, perhaps the most difficult is taking account of the complex implications of this fact and enabling others to recognize its importance. Imagine being the facilitator in this scenario:

> *When Robert wanted to have more say about how he lived his life, it was difficult for him to express it for fear of hurting his mother's feelings. His bi-polar disorder had made it difficult in the past for people around him to hear what he really wanted. He felt his mother was overprotective and that others often saw his diagnosis first, rather than who he really was. What he really wanted was to move out of his mother's home and live on his own. The facilitator started by helping Robert identify people he loved and who loved him. He called it the 'You Matter' list. It included his mother, his uncle, the preacher and two neighbours. The facilitator then helped Robert identify which of those people he wanted to help him with decision making. His uncle and one neighbour were on this list.*

His mother was not. Robert was nervous about telling his mother that he didn't want her on the decision-making list, but only on the 'You Matter' list. He didn't want a confrontation or to upset her. The facilitator helped Robert make a video explaining why his mother is so important to him, but also why he chose two other people for help with decision making. He gave the video to his mother before his next planning meeting. With Robert's agreement, the facilitator offered to sit with the mother while she watched. While it's still a struggle at times for both Robert and his mother, the choice of his decision-making support has been respected.

It could not have been easy for the facilitator, but she had an understanding of and commitment to Robert's autonomy, so she did not take the easy road.

- It would have been easier to suggest to Robert that it would be less stressful to include his mother on his decision-making list. Instead the facilitator helped Robert use his voice to explain his decision to his mother.

- It would have been easier not to ask Robert to make distinctions between people that matter and those he actually wanted to help him make decisions. Instead the facilitator knew that having to think this through would increase Robert's sense of his autonomy.

- It would have been easier to continue to assume that Robert's mother would be a key decision maker in his life. Instead the facilitator focused on Robert.

The facilitator held strongly to the principle of self-determination even when it was difficult.

When self-determination is discussed, decision making of a person's family is often used interchangeably with decision making of that person. Facilitators in the New Story value and validate all ideas, thoughts and opinions but never lose the 'self' in self-determination.

Facilitators value and validate all ideas, thoughts and opinions but never lose the 'self' in self-determination.

Facilitators use their facilitation skills to recognize and respond to autonomy in many different situations:

- When a family believes their aging parents' dementia negates their right to any decision-making …the facilitator helps the family find creative ways to support the voice and choice of that person.

- When a husband believes his wife's mental health issues mean she shouldn't make any parenting decisions …the facilitator supports the husband and wife to figure out a process of parenting that enables the wife to be as engaged as possible.

- When staff in a residential service believe that a person who does not use verbal language cannot make choices …the facilitator supports the staff and that person to design a system of communication that enables his or her choices to be heard and honoured.

It is not unusual for families or service providers to take control of a situation and to act on the judgement of what they think is in the best interest of the person. While this is usually well intentioned, it can stem from low expectations and a reflection of love: it can be a continuation of long-standing roles in a parent-child relationship, or be based on fear of what might go wrong and a desire to keep the person safe. Facilitators recognize when this is happening and help others see it as well. We raise awareness, gently steer, and create conditions to have open and honest conversations. Like Robert's mother, many people need strategies and encouragement to move from directing and guiding to listening and supporting what someone believes is important to him or her personally.

> " *It's very hard when everyone assumes that family will make decisions for a family member. Helping them move from "What do you want for your loved one?" to "What do you think they would want for themselves?" can be one of the toughest things to facilitate.* "

If someone tells us we are working too much, we can push back verbally and continue to act on our own judgement. But if, for example, Jeff is drinking too much Coke ("it's bad for his teeth") and he can't push back in a way that can be heard by those around him, typically the decision is made by others who are then exerting control over him. Facilitators help people think beyond a simple solution like hiding the Coke from Jeff (a solution all too often used). They ask deeper questions about how Jeff can have control over his life, his choices, and honour his family's desire that Jeff be healthy (drinking through a straw limits sugar left on the teeth, 'diet' drinks don't contain cavity-inducing sugars, etc.) The facilitator structures these conversations with those concerned so they too can learn to respect, appreciate, and support self-determination.

In terms of autonomy, *noticing* is critical for facilitators:

Many people need strategies and encouragement to move from directing and guiding to listening and supporting what the person believes is important to them personally.

- is this person's voice central or are others speaking 'for' that person?

- is this person making genuine personal decisions or are decisions getting made 'in the person's best interest'?

- is the facilitation process at a pace and level of content that is comfortable for this person or are others driving it to be 'efficient'?

- is the facilitation process one that provides this person with more experience with decision making or is the person being protected from building experience with decision making?

Compliance Doesn't Work

Patricia Deegan, international mental health recovery advocate, asks important questions about the paradox of compliance:

> *Do we work in a system which rewards passivity, obedience and compliance? Is compliance seen as a desirable outcome? As a friend who is a consumer/survivor told me, "Tell those case managers that they have it all wrong. Tell them to stop saying that compliance is the road to independence." And indeed, compliance is not the road to independence. Learning to become self-determining is an outcome that is indicative of environments that support opportunities for recovery and empowerment.[11]*

Our formal systems of care have been dominated by compliance and carrot-and

-stick approaches, which social science literature has shown to be less effective than approaches which stress self-determination.

The Doorway Project in Calgary was founded in 1988 as an experiment in social change. The initial goal was to test a cost-effective method of assisting long-term street youth (aged 17 – 24) in moving to mainstream society. Their belief statement is:

> *Every person has the right to a self-constructed life. This freedom is founded and nurtured from within, and is learned from the context of our lives.*

The methodology of the Doorway Project was developed as an alternative to the increasing costs of traditional programs, which foster dependence rather than nurture independence. What emerged from this pilot project was a non-traditional approach that boasts a consistently high success rate.[12]

Similarly, several states in the U.S. that have implemented self-determination projects for the last decade have found very positive results when people with developmental disabilities are supported to have genuine choice and control in their everyday lives. The Florida Self-Directed Care program defines choice as "the ability and opportunity to select between alternatives, to have a say in the choice made, and to have options." Better quality of life outcomes result from such practices, and research is showing that such initiatives are highly cost effective.[13]

Facilitators Open Up Spaces

Facilitators ensure the opportunity for others around a person to witness and acknowledge the person's growth in decision making.

Skilful facilitators always bring people back to the idea of personhood. Taking the person we are working with seriously, as an autonomous individual with opinions and the capacity to grow and develop, acknowledges who they are now and who they can emerge to be. Facilitators watch for any lack of faith in the person's ability to make decisions and then create conversation about how that undermines self-determination. We ensure opportunity for others around the person to witness and support his or her growth as a decision maker. It may start with seemingly small steps. But it must start with everyday life experiences. We know that success builds on success. Doesn't self-determination begin when we are trusted to act? It begins as children and continues life-long.

Facilitators are continually opening up spaces for people to build experience, confidence, and competence in decision making. This often begins by supporting the little decisions that we all need to make in everyday life. For some people, this may

> *Facilitators are continually opening up spaces for people to build experience, confidence, and competence in decision making.*

mean doing their own banking for the first time. For others, it may mean planning menus and shopping for food for the first time. For still others it may be respecting and responding to their use of the word 'no'.

When facilitators are opening up spaces for people to make decisions, they also need to make sure they are asking questions that are linked with experience and information. If we ask someone who has never lived anywhere but in the family home whether they want to live in an apartment, they may have no frame of reference. If we ask questions outside of their experience, it is unfair. If we ask someone who is homeless if they want to go to the hospital and it's never been a welcoming place, it is unfair. Facilitators make sure that their questions are framed in a way that makes it possible to move forward. They might ask questions that help people identify what they like or don't like about living in the family home, or questions about how they might feel safe getting medical help.

Facilitators also help everyone understand that self-determination is more than "I want..." Facilitators help people understand the work involved in living the life they choose. More than just "I want," there is also:

- *I can decide...*
- *I can choose...*
- *I can create...*
- *I can ask others...*
- *I am responsible...*
- *I contribute...*
- *I participate...*
- *I can be intentional...*
- *I know the impact...*

> " *When we ask people questions outside of their experience, it may be too easy to conclude that their response is indicative of their inability to make decisions.* "

Assessing Self-Determination

☐ I decide whether to live alone or with someone else.
☐ I control who can and can't come into my home.
☐ I can choose where I live.
☐ I choose my own friends.
☐ I decide whether or not to have a boyfriend or girlfriend.
☐ I have people in my life who respect my values and choices.
☐ I decide how to be part of my community.
☐ If I want to go somewhere, transportation isn't a problem.
☐ I'm able to stand up for myself to get what I need.
☐ My basic human rights are respected.
☐ I'm free to choose the kinds of goals I want to pursue.
☐ I freely choose what kinds of medical treatment I get.
☐ I have the final say over how I spend my money.
☐ I know how to deal with prejudice and discrimination.

Express Yourself:
Assessing Self-Determination in Your Life
National Research and Training Center on Psychiatric Disability

Over time, as people experience choice and control over their own environment and everyday life, they are more likely to include more than 'I want' in expressing how they would like to live. In the chart above, the National Research and Training Center on Psychiatric Disability outlines ways that people can assess their own self-determination.

Self-Determination Is More Than Just Talk

What if a person is unable to use language to communicate? Is that a reason to say self-determination can't be realized? Limited forms of communication have restricted people's lives and decision making and led to an assumption that people who don't talk do not have anything to say.

Self-determination becomes the expression of self and is linked with having an identity in community life.

Human beings are designed neurologically to engage and be active in their own lives.

Scientists at Bloorview Kids Rehab in Toronto have developed a prototype device that allows a kind of mind-reading, using near-infrared light, to decipher the brain's response when a person is offered a choice of two objects. A computer is used to recognize the unique pattern of brain activity associated with preference.[14] Tom Chau, a senior scientist at Bloorview, was quoted as saying that the mind is alert in people robbed of communication skills. This is a compelling argument that people who do not communicate formally do have preferences and the brain is active in forming preferences – whether they can be expressed or not. In other words, people's receptive language is far better than their expressive language. Facilitators may need to remind people of that. As facilitators, it means we may have to listen differently. We may have to pay attention to actions, not just words. We may have to sit in silence together. It means we must take the time to understand before we move to decision making. And then we may have to help those around a person listen differently, and learn together to be creative in the ways we explore the world with people who do not communicate with words.

As facilitators, it means we may have to listen differently. We may have to pay attention to actions, not just words. We may have to sit in silence together. It means we must take the time to understand before we move to decision making.

Part of this involves recognizing the types of communication that work best for a person and helping others become comfortable with different ways of listening: facial expressions, eye movements, relaxing or tensing parts of the body, and vocalizations.

We also look for clues in the family and community culture. People may communicate in different ways in their church community, at a community sports event, and around the family dinner table. We become observers and help others to observe as well. We are looking for patterns of behaviour that indicate choice making. We are looking for clues in the environment about personal preferences and we are asking those who love this person to speak from the heart about what that person wants and needs in order to live a meaningful life.

Facilitators are looking for clues in the environment about personal preferences and we are asking those who love this person to speak from the heart about what that person wants and needs in order to live a meaningful life.

Facilitators Understand the Power of Purpose

Research on how people best learn shows that autonomy and purpose are central to learning and development. People have to feel that they have control in their lives and have a sense of purpose. We learn

We learn better when we are given freedom to decide on what is meaningful for us.

better when we are given freedom to decide on what is meaningful for us. As Daniel Pink's research shows, autonomy and purpose together are highly motivating.[15]

Facilitators understand there that is power in purpose. We all seek purpose that is personally meaningful. We help people deepen their autonomy and confidence by exploring their own purpose and meaning.

> *Carl loves words and writes poetry whenever he can. When Carl was recovering from a serious stroke, the facilitator encouraged him to express his thoughts and feelings through poetry. Eventually, with the assistance of his facilitator, and the support of a small poetry group, Carl self-published a small book of poetry and began to read his poems at a library poetry circle. His self-confidence and sense of autonomy grew during this process.*

Carl may not have described his experience as deepening his autonomy and sense of purpose, but it was evident in his willingness to share his poetry journal with others. His facilitator noticed and nurtured Carl's renewed sense of purpose and personal growth. In turn, he encouraged others in Carl's life to notice and nurture it as well.

Supported Decision Making

One of the struggles people face is not just their presumed incompetence to make decisions (without a finding of incompetence by the courts), but a lack of support of their legal capacity to do so. Legal capacity is a term that basically means the ability to engage in a legal process, like enter into a contract. It includes the legal right to speak on one's own behalf. It assumes an ability to comprehend both the nature and consequences of one's acts.[16]

In Canada we have usually dealt with a person's inability to comprehend by appointing someone to make decisions for that person. This substitute decision maker takes over the legal capacity of a person, assuming a role referred to as *guardianship*. It makes people particularly vulnerable when they are found incapable of exercising their legal rights. They are deprived of these rights entirely when their rights are transferred to guardians.

The United Nations Convention on the Rights of Persons with Disabilities makes an insightful and significant change in how we support people in their decision-making. Rather than act "in the best interest of" people through guardianship and substitute decision making, the Convention (Article 12) places an obligation on governments to provide support to assist people with disabilities in exercising their own decision-making capacity. It says people have the right to have the support they need to make their own decisions. Canada ratified the Convention on March 11, 2010. And although Canada reserved the right to continue the use of substitute decision-making arrangements in appropriate circumstances, hopefully the intent of Article 12 will be honoured in the day to day lives of all people.

This is a tremendous opportunity for facilitators! We can help create and ensure supportive decision-making environments for people who have not had a voice in the decisions that affect their lives. It must begin with presumed competence. It must begin with relationships and networks of people who can rally around someone to support this person to make his or her own decisions. However it happens, it must begin.

And there is a role for everyone in creating supportive decision-making environments. Facilitators are responsible for ensuring that those roles are understood, embraced and honoured.

Families can usually provide insight into strategies that work in communicating with a family member (most obviously for those who do not express themselves with words, but for others as well). The facilitator learns from the family and provides opportunities for successful strategies to be shared with the broader network. Families also often give voice to safety and security concerns. The facilitator helps in this situation to ensure the

> *There is a role for everyone in creating supportive decision-making environments. Facilitators are responsible for ensuring that those roles are understood, embraced and honoured.*

"best guess" focuses on the will of the person and considers past experience and observation.

Networks of family and friends can ensure that a person's voice is listened to in all decisions. There may be times when people in the person's network are not able to understand what choice the person wants. When it is a 'best guess' of what the person wants, the network takes responsibility for making that decision and documenting why and how they feel that is what the person was expressing or would have expressed. The facilitator helps networks to listen deeply, take their time, and be creative in supporting the person's voice and choice.

Service agencies can assist each person who uses their support to develop and/ or maintain their own decision-making process. And they should act on the decisions made through such a process. The process should take into account how each person communicates and who in the person's life helps them with decision making.

Self-determination may also get defined differently over time as a person's circumstances change and as a person grows. Michael Kennedy, disability advocate, says:

> *The meaning of self-determination has changed for me over the years. When I was in the institutions, I had to make sure I got the basic care I needed, like my personal hygiene and three meals a day, so that was what self-determination meant at that time. There, the caregivers seemed to think people didn't know what they wanted or how they wanted it done. Now, self-determination means running my own life and directing my personal care assistants on how best to assist me... Now, people treat me like a human being who knows what I want and who needs support to live my life. They ask me what I want and how I want it done. They also ask me what is the easiest way to get things done, so that I feel comfortable and they feel comfortable as well. So self-determination doesn't mean you have to do everything yourself, but it does mean you have to be in charge of your life to the fullest extent that you possibly can be.*[17]

Balancing Self-Determination and Community

In recent years, self-determination and community have emerged as two of the key values that are guiding independent facilitation. In the past, philosophers often saw these values as opposites – one is about *I*, while the other is about *we*. Facilitators understand that both are central in building rich, everyday lives in community. Without self-determination, opportunities for choice and growth are significantly limited. On the other hand, without community, people have limited opportunity for relationships and participation.

> *When facilitators cast the net to include more people, it increases the likelihood that balance can be found between self-determination and community.*

Facilitators also understand that self-determination and community sometimes collide. A person's self-determined choices may not be acceptable to the family or the neighbourhood. Or the community may be intolerant of behaviour or actions of this person. At these times, the facilitator must be skilful in bringing the right people together to find common ground. The first question to explore is often "who needs to be involved in this issue?" When we cast the net to include more people, it increases the likelihood that balance can be found between self-determination and community. Another question that may need to be explored is "what are the intentions here?" This question enables people to explore differences, but ultimately presses them to find common ground. Facilitators understand that participation is central to finding balance between self-determination and community.

Self-Determination is Central to Social Movements

In the last decade, self-determination has been recognized as a key part of social movements across North America. Facilitators appreciate how self-determination is becoming a beacon for people who have traditionally not had voice in our communities. In Canada, the importance of self-determination as a value is reflected within several social movements, all with the expressed purpose of enhancing rights and citizenship.

The Independent Living movement in Canada has worked within an empowerment framework for almost thirty years. People with disabilities are reclaiming personal

Components of Self-Determination

Freedom: The right to make basic choices about your life. Does everyone helping this person make decisions believe they have a right to make basic choices about their life?

Authority: To control the money that is spent on your behalf for the supports you receive. Support agreements must be developed together by individuals and funders. Funds must be assigned to individuals rather than slots. People with disabilities must be allowed to use those funds to purchase the supports they require. They also must be able to personally select (hire) and direct people who provide support or assistance.

Support: To organize resources in ways that are life enhancing and meaningful to the individual. Each person who experiences disability can determine the supports that work for him or her. People with disabilities (together with those they trust, if they want) have the right to figure out their life goals, what kind of supports might work, and how to make and keep track of plans and budgets.

Responsibility: To give back to your community and be accountable for the wise use of public dollars. People with disabilities have the responsibility to fulfill the ordinary obligations of citizenship like obeying laws, directing their own lives, participating in community life, and voting.

Confirmation: Of the important leadership role that individuals with disabilities and families play in a newly re-designed system and through their support for the advocacy movement.

Center for Self-Determination
www.centerforself-determination.com

power, which is supported in thirty Independent Living Centres across the country. Self-determination is a key principle of the Independent Living movement. Consumer control is reflected in several attendant service projects, where people get to decide what kind of support they require, when it should be provided, and how it should be provided.[18]

In the community mental health field, *recovery* is becoming a dominant value. Recovery advocates believe that people with significant mental health issues should experience conditions that focus on self-determination and participation.

The Recovery model emphasizes and supports each individual's potential for recovery and recognizes that people's involvement is critical to the prospects for success. Research is showing that *recovery* approaches can lead to very positive quality of life outcomes.[19]

In the developmental disability field, the People First self-advocacy movement has strong roots in Canada and the United States. People First was formed because people felt that they were not seen

Canadian Charter of Rights

15 (1) Every individual is equal before and under the law and has the right to the equal protection and equal benefit of the law without discrimination and, in particular, without discrimination based on race, national or ethnic origin, colour, religion, sex, age or mental or physical disability.

as persons, but only as a disability label. People First in Canada have been strong proponents of self-determination. Resources developed by People First of Canada reflect people's strong desire to be able to choose a life that is personally meaningful. [20]

The poverty-reduction movement has been growing across Canada. Led by the Vital Communities Initiative, work in poverty reduction is also grounded in self-determination and community. Several regions of Canada are building the capacity of families by engaging facilitators to work directly with families living with low incomes. Facilitators who do this work support families to consider their own capacity, engage them in change strategies, and help families think about new ways of accessing resources.[21]

Professional practice in the field of elder abuse prevention is guided by principles that highlight individual freedom and civil liberties. In working with victims and vulnerable persons, professionals look for ways to prevent abuse that promote autonomy and self-determination.[22]

The recent thrust in these self-determination movements is not about fighting for legal rights (that battle was won in 1982 with the Canadian Charter of Rights). It is about social movements encouraging communities and governments to recognize and honour the rights that all Canadians already have. As facilitators, we understand this thrust and are aware of social movements in our local communities that might serve as a resource to the people we support. Self-determination is a central value guiding our work as facilitators in order for others to claim an everyday life.

Standing Still to Move Ahead

For facilitators, self-determination means walking with people on their life journeys as they gain experience in expressing their voice and choices. It also means assisting others to support those choices even when they differ from their own opinions. As we stand still, we become aware how we, and others, often 'decide for' or 'do for' the other person. We also might notice how people may struggle with "letting go" so they too can support self-determination. We help others notice these things too.

We are supporting people to become engaged in sculpting their own lives. As facilitators in the self-determination process, we are opening space for people to gain experience and explore possibilities from which to make decisions. As we stand still, we notice that people may have to make a major shift toward self-determination in order to build an everyday life in community.

As you reflect on the ways in which you support self-determination, consider when and where you struggle with the idea and the process. What conditions seem to make the process easier?

Chapter Five

Getting to Know People and Their Context

In our culture, there is a strong tendency to make assumptions about people based on groups they belong to. For disadvantaged groups, many are negative. Think about the stereotypes and myths about people who are homeless, people with mental health issues, or families coping with poverty. It is difficult to imagine how people can lead everyday lives if they are bogged down battling these negative assumptions. It is often only through getting to know people as individuals that those assumptions melt away.

Facilitators not only resist the tendency to be directed by negative assumptions, we proactively support the development of positive identities. Facilitators can only do that by getting to know someone. And we can only get to know someone if a relationship has been developed.

In developing a relationship, facilitators learn about people's strengths, as well as their hopes and dreams. As we are getting to know someone, we are moving beyond assumptions about need, circumstance, or disability. We also take time to get to know the person's context, both their social and physical environments and how it impacts their lives. This is critical to helping people define what they want their everyday lives to look like.

Taking Time

Facilitators are getting to know a person beyond the assumptions about need, circumstance or disability.

Time. It is often a struggle to have enough, but it is vital for facilitators to take the time to get to know people: their strengths, hopes and fears, what they find motivating or discouraging, what is important, what they want and what they need. We must take time to understand people's life experiences and the various contexts in which they live, work, and participate. What we learn by doing so acts as a guide for engaging people, asking the right questions, ensuring the right support is in place for the facilitation process, and ensuring that they can make positive change in their own lives to become the best they can be. Helping someone answer the question, "Who am I?" often leads that person to ask "Who can I become?" and "Who do I want to become?"

Facilitators learn about people in a variety of ways – through conversation, stories, observation, participation in shared activities, and through the eyes and, sometimes, the hearts of others. Exploring ideas with a small group or 'circle' of people chosen by the person we are working with is often a powerful way to get to know someone.[23] All of these approaches create opportunities to discover the essence of someone's identity.

Facilitators may also get to know and establish a relationship with someone by exploring things together in the community. This enables us to deepen our understanding of people and their contexts.

Jake has always loved music and the facilitator and Jake went to the library for the first time. As they explored the library's collection of DVDs, the facilitator deepened his appreciation of Jake's love of music and his knowledge of several music genres. The facilitator paid attention to what Jake was drawn to, his conversation with the librarian, and how his energy changed when he talked about certain music. By being together in the community Jake helped the facilitator get to know him. The facilitator, in turn, observed Jake and thought about possibilities in other areas of the community.

Facilitators understand that getting to know a person and their community is "inside out" work. It does not happen by reading a file or hearing a professional give an assessment. It happens when a person allows us to see who they are, to share insights about their hopes and longings, and to enable us to gain awareness of the struggles they are experiencing. Facilitators also recognize that their understanding of a person might change over time: a man who previously lived on the streets and who now has a home is a different person than he was before.

Getting to Know Strengths

Facilitation is strengths-based work. Facilitators are always looking for assets in individuals, families, networks, and neighbourhoods. It has become a cliché that strengths are important in person-centred work. Yet even though the importance of strengths is recognized all around, oftentimes people simply create a list of strengths in one meeting. We know that we cannot possibly get to know a person in such a short time.

We begin with three assumptions about strengths:

- *Everyone has strengths to share.*

- *It is possible to find places and spaces in the community to share strengths.*

- *It takes time to discover genuine strengths.*

We must be patient in getting to know a person. Imagine if we rushed this piece of facilitation and were wrong about a person's strengths. It could lead to helping someone de-

Facilitators take their time to be sure insights are accurate.

velop a life plan based on a false impression. Because so much of what facilitators do is based on knowing the person, we take our time to be sure insights are accurate.

When Miranda was leaving high school, a facilitator spent some time with Miranda and her family exploring things that she might do as a young adult. During one planning conversation, the facilitator asked

> *As people expand their relationships, what they imagine for their future may change. As people increase their community connections, their skills and interests may grow. As people gain more life experience, their expectations will expand.*

Miranda if she liked animals. She responded with a cautious "yes", and this interest was recorded. On the next visit, the facilitator said she knew someone who owned a pet store and Miranda could apply to do some part-time work there. After several weeks on the job, Miranda told her family that she hated the animals at the pet store. When she had told the facilitator she liked animals, she really meant that she likes petting the neighbour's cat because that's when the neighbour chats with her for long periods of time.

While facilitators are aware of the dangers of early errors, we are open and flexible enough to adapt to the idea that a person and family will change over time. As people expand their relationships, what they imagine for their future may change. As people increase their community connections, their skills and interests may grow. As people gain more life experience, their expectations will expand.

Deficits and weaknesses are often the focus of services and society in general. Imagine planning for your own retirement. Would you be able to plan a meaningful retirement life if you based your planning on deficits and weaknesses? Can you imagine how discouraging such a list would be? How can someone thinking about reclaiming an everyday life build that life only on a list of needs?

Facilitators think of strengths in four inter-related ways: skills, interests, talents, and gifts.

Skills as Strengths

We all have skills which we have learned over the years. Most of us are continuing to develop skills at each stage of our lives. Facilitators understand people's skills and create opportunities to use those skills and develop new skills. For example, Marcel wants to increase his computer literacy, and the facilitator connects him with someone at the local Independent Living

> *Facilitators understand people's skills and create opportunities to use those skills and develop new skills.*

Centre. Most Centres across Canada either provide computer literacy training or they support local computer groups to include people with disabilities.

Interests as Strengths

Our interests reflect our passions and what is characteristic of us as people. Some people love to cook and see it as an expression of their creative selves. Other people love outdoor hiking and camping and see it as an expression of their close connection with nature. Some people may

We also understand that people need to experience life to discover their interests. We notice environments where interests are expressed.

never have had the opportunity to explore their interests. This can take time and requires facilitators to intentionally listen to what interests them. We also understand that people need to expand their life experiences to discover their interests. We notice and encourage interests in environments where they emerge.

Talents as Strengths

Talents are skills or assets for which we have a particular aptitude. Children often show an early talent for music, art, or dance. Like skills, talents need to be nurtured and supported in order to fully develop. Research shows that talents are unrelated to intelligence and are more accessible to people

Facilitators notice people's talents and we encourage their development if they want to pursue them.

than originally thought. Facilitators notice people's talents and we encourage their development if they want to pursue them. Often it is a matter of allowing time and space for the talent to emerge and be supported.

Discovering and Nurturing Gifts

The notion of people having gifts has emerged in recent years. There are two distinct meanings to the word 'gift' in this sort of discussion. One meaning suggests that we all have gifts, but that what makes us unique is our *core* gift. Someone may have several gifts (compassion, playing the piano, and public speaking), but their core

Three Kinds of Gifts

Each type of gift reflects a person's identity, although people may experience all types of gifts at various times.

Gift of Presence means that a person's presence is enough to engender hospitality or relationship. Certain people can light up a room with their smile. Facilitators notice places in community where people can be present and included and where their gift of presence can shine. Facilitators ask, "What happens to others in the presence of this person?"

Gift of Participation means that people's participation in community life is an expression of their interests and strengths. Participation can range from recreation and leisure to politics and civic engagement. Facilitators notice possibilities for community participation based on interests and strengths. Facilitators ask, "Who in community needs this gift?"

Gift of Contribution means that people are contributing their gift to the community and beyond. Many people with disabilities, for example, are contributing to issues 'beyond disability' whether as a teacher, a politician, an artist, a motivational speaker, or as an entrepreneur. Facilitators notice how they can support people to move from disability consumers to community leaders. Facilitators ask, "What places can appreciate this gift?"

This framework is adapted from John Lord and Peggy Hutchison, *Pathways to Inclusion: Building a New Story with People and Communities*. Concord, ON: Captus Press, Second edition, 2011.

gift may be "using music and words to inspire people to care about mother earth." In this sense, our core gift reflects our interests, talents, and passions, and also our uniqueness.

Another meaning of gifts refers to the broad spectrum of *human* gifts. These types of gifts often include sensitivity, leadership, compassion, service, and organization. In this sense, we can say that we all have gifts, but they vary quite considerably from person to person. Facilitators understand that gifts are not always what they seem. For example, Jenine is a young woman who uses a wheelchair and does not use words to express herself. Yet her infectious smile and engaging personality gives her the gift of hospitality that few others bring to relationships. Some people may express one characteristic that is a compelling gift. Others may have a range of strengths that we think of as gifts.

As we are getting to know a person and his or her interests, skills, and talents, we are identifying themes that reflect what gifts this person may have. These themes capture the essence of who this person is, his or her gift or gifts. Here are some statements that people have created about their own gift in collaboration with a facilitator:

> "I can build community through movement. I know this because my dancing brings people together in dance and laughter."

> "My gift is energy. I know this because my energy inspires others to become energetic and creative."

Bruce Anderson, author of *The Teacher's Gift,* has created a very powerful template for facilitators to explore gifts.[24] He outlines how critical it is to use dialogue, ask good questions, and seek clarification as part of guided conversation. Anderson suggests that to really get at our gifts, we need to see what emerges when exploring skills, talents, and interests. He points out that deeper work is also needed because our gifts usually cross over our interests and talents. These also reflect the deeper motivations that underlie our patterns and activity preferences.

Anderson describes several kinds of conversations to discover gifts:

- Imagine you are having a conversation with a good friend about your gifts. What might they say about your gifts? What do they think you contribute to the world? This helps us imagine our gifts through the eyes of others.

- Explore what in your life has been meaningful for you. When have you felt most fulfilled? What and where have you contributed over and over again? What is a dominant passion that keeps playing over and over? This kind of conversation helps us to learn about personal meaning.

- Explore what you have learned through difficulties in your life. What did you learn about yourself during times of adversity? What strengths and insights have you noticed during challenging times in your life? This approach helps us to explore vulnerability, since it is often at these times that we gain self-awareness.

Facilitators must remember that we are not using a gifts approach in order to give a person another label. Facilitators explore gifts so that a person can use their strengths in their community to move towards the vision they have for their own life. A case in point, a person who discovers that they have an aptitude for teaching can be supported to become a teacher, in whatever area is important to that person.

The process of exploring gifts weaves in and out of the relationship we have with an individual or family. It is never a one-time activity, but is part of the journey of deepening insight over time. The process of discovering and nurturing gifts increases confidence. "I am good at…", I am appreciated for…", I can do this…" are statements we might hear as people deepen their awareness of their own gifts.

This work is strongly supported by research on the empowerment process.[25] As people gain more personal control and increase participation in their lives, research shows that they experience more self-efficacy. They become more aware of their own skills and capacities. Facilitators understand the power and importance of supporting the empowerment process. Enabling people to discover and nurture their gifts is central to this process.

Imagining a Better Everyday Life

Karen had been doing yoga for about six years. She loved the movement and was known by her teacher as being "in the moment." Karen is very flexible with her body and had been growing in confidence in her yoga practice. Several times over a period of months, Karen quietly said at family gatherings, "I want to be a yoga teacher." Although some family members heard the whispers, no one responded, perhaps because of the assumption they had of Karen that did not include her being a yoga teacher. However, when a new facilitator began to work with Karen, the facilitator immediately noticed Karen's quiet intention to be a yoga teacher. The facilitator saw only possibility and helped those who love Karen to get excited about Karen's journey to become a yoga teacher.

People who have not yet claimed their everyday life may have little experience in imagining that life could be any different than it is today. Although this is often the case, it is equally true that others who know a person often do not hear the 'whispers' that are expressed as a desire for change. Karen's facilitator paid attention to the quiet whispers and helped others to hear and support them as well. As Stephen Cassetari, author of *Reflections on the River* has written, "You can only get there from here."[26] By focusing on the 'now' as our starting point, we notice the patterns and intentions that people show in their daily lives. And as we get to know people, we usually learn more about their hopes and desires. Many people refer to this as *discovering dreams*. As facilitators working in a New Story, we want to unearth more than just what someone fancies. We want to assist people to unleash their imagination as they picture themselves in everyday life.

As Albert Einstein said, "Your imagination is your preview of life's coming attractions." Imagination can bring us to a new level of thinking about the future. It is like a spiral, building and building on ideas and creativity. While building, it may change and reshape how we think about our future. Facilitators encourage people to dream and to be imaginative about their lives, and to welcome the reshaping that happens when imagining a future.

Facilitators understand that what people imagine for themselves can take various forms and be expressed in a variety of ways:

I hope...

I desire...

I strive...

I intend...

I pursue...

I inspire...

I can...

I imagine…

> " *We have to listen to the whispers. Sometimes people around the person have low expectations and need a translator, who can remind them of the voice and dreams of the person.* "

We have hopes about many things in our lives. The idea of imagining change is not meant to limit us but instead to expand possibility: for relationships, participation and contribution. These intentions and longings often serve as catalysts to begin thinking in a new way or to have a new conversation.

Laurie's support circle always buys a lottery ticket before each meeting. It is not so much because they are counting on winning (although that would be nice) but the ticket serves two purposes. It stimulates conversation – "If I won...," and is also a reminder that everyone has dreams and can imagine themselves in a different future. It also shows that relationships with others can inform our own future. We may expand our own imagination by hearing about the creativity and resourcefulness of others.

Facilitators have a role in helping people express their future in ways that lead to action. We ask questions that enable people to deepen their own insights and to connect them with others in their network.

- What is it about imagining a new future that excites you?
- Who else shares this with you?
- What people will understand and appreciate what you have imagined for yourself?
- What places can welcome and strengthen you as you make changes in your life?

Imagining change is built on current reality, and facilitators find ways to shift or change that reality. The Dalai Lama says, "If you want a community of joy, full of friends, you should create that possibility... If you want a more friendly neighbourhood, you must create the atmosphere."[27] In other words, imagining a new tomorrow is only the beginning. Facilitators assist people in actualizing their dreams by ambitiously pursuing an everyday life of their own choosing.

Facilitators Understand Context

Human beings like to generalize. We use generalizations to assist us with all kinds of decision making: in general, there is more traffic at 5 pm than there is at 2 pm. In general, Joe is a reliable person and I can count on him to complete the job.

Yet, facilitators understand that generalizing can lead to stereotyping that is not helpful. Mary has some challenging behaviours, so we assume that Mary cannot change. Similarly, the fact that a person demonstrates a strength in one setting does not mean they will show that same strength in all settings.

Facilitators resist generalizing because we understand the power of context. Research shows that we typically underestimate the role that context plays in people's behaviour.[28] For example, when the facilitator met with Mate in the coffee shop, he felt he was getting to know a confident young man, who was clear about his aspirations. When the facilitator met Mate at home with his parents, he encountered a shy, passive person, who let his parents talk for him. This kind of 'context difference' is not unusual, but it highlights the importance of facilitators taking time to get to know someone in different contexts.

We support people to ask others about possible places and people that would understand the dream. This expands people's relationships beyond themselves and creates a range of conversations about the dream and how it might be expressed or experienced.

Community contexts and places are where people express and experience their dreams. Place matters to what we hope for our future. A community place will either dampen a dream or amplify the dream. Part of our role as facilitators is to enable people to find places that are a good fit with what they imagine for themselves. We support people to ask others about possible places and people that would understand the dream. This expands people's relationships beyond themselves and creates a range of conversations about the dream and how it might be expressed or experienced.

Getting to Know People Never Ends

Getting to know people involves listening with understanding. As part of this process, facilitators are always looking for strengths and how they can be expressed. We also pay attention to people's hopes and what they imagine for their future, and provide support that enables them to be expressed.

We also get to know people in a variety of contexts so they can deepen their understanding of themselves and become connected with a range of people and places. We use our craft in such a way that each person can create an everyday life rich in relationships, using their strengths and dreams to contribute to their community in their own way.

Standing Still to Move Ahead

Getting to know another person takes time. As we stand still, we notice that our role is like a mirror for that person. We provide questions and space that enable people to discover what they already know, but perhaps have not had the opportunity or conditions to bring to the fore. As strengths and dreams emerge, we become aware that this work cannot happen in isolation. The insights and possibilities increase many fold when we invite others to be part of the journey. Bringing in other perspectives enriches the person and the process. In this way, we realize that finding people and places that would understand what someone imagines for their future is a vital part of our work as facilitators.

When we stand still, we also learn that our own strengths and dreams matter. When we notice ourselves, and what we may imagine, we deepen our sensitivity and possibilities as facilitators. We also discover those places of resistance within ourselves.

Understanding our own personal journey, including our struggles with adversity, gives us insights into ourselves in ways that strengthen our ability to assist others. As you reflect on ways that you have come to know yourself over the years, what can you learn that might be helpful to the facilitation work you do?

Chapter Six

Embracing the Richness of Community

Community can conjure up a romantic notion of earlier times, when towns and villages seemed to provide a sense of belonging and genuine hospitality. Facilitators know that community affords tremendous possibilities for experiencing participation, contribution, and social inclusion. A community is a group of people who have learned to (mostly) get along together and share some common norms. Communities are all around us and part of us, in family, in neighbourhood, in workplaces, or in organizations. Facilitators know that the right supports can enable people to be part of all of these kinds of community life.

We know that being part of a community can be an exhilarating experience when we feel welcomed and when our participation is nurtured and valued. We also know that being part of a community can be a negative experience for people, when rights are denied and barriers to participation seem insurmountable. Community life can also be harmful when community norms are narrowly defined and place emphasis on exclusion.

Facilitators understand the complex fabric of community and see potential and possibility everywhere. We know that the heart of community is about citizenship.

Facilitators understand the complex fabric of community and see potential and possibility everywhere. We know that the heart of community is citizenship. And citizenship is about participation, belonging, and contributing.

Robert Putnam, influential academic and author of *Bowling Alone*, found that: "*School performance, public health, crime rates, clinical depression, tax compliance, philanthropy, race relations, community development, census returns, teen suicide, economic productivity, campaign finance, even simple human happiness — all are demonstrably affected by how (and whether) we connect with our family and friends and neighbours and co-workers.*"[29] Putnam explores the concept of social capital, first described in the early 1900s, as "connections among individuals – social networks and the norms of reciprocity and trustworthiness that arise from them." Putnam is one of many who recognize the importance of social capital. Facilitators also recognize this rich resource is only to be found in the relationships that make up community life.

Facilitators embrace the community principle: community as a first resort. Community as a first resort means that facilitators always think of community first when they are supporting someone to build an everyday life. Think how powerful this principle can be! When a person needs a home, we think of all the possibilities in the community. When a person needs relationships, we think of friends, family, and community members yet unmet. When a person needs a cup of sugar, we think first of borrowing from a neighbour. We might well explore formal supports and services with someone, but only when these supports enhance an everyday life.

> *Community as a first resort means that facilitators always think of community first when they are supporting someone to build an everyday life.*

A Story of Community

There is well known research on the community of Rosetta, Pennsylvania, in the United States that shows that people in this community live longer, have fewer health problems, and generally reported experiencing a very good quality of life. Researchers could not find any explanation for this incredible difference with other communities. They then began to notice the daily patterns of the residents of this community.

After work, it was not unusual for people to have long conversations on their porches or spend time together in various places throughout the community. Observers noted that there was a strong 'sense of community'. People often gathered for pot-luck dinners, and food and hospitality were known to go hand in hand. Researchers discovered that community members were experiencing strong connections with one another.[30]

As early as 1978, research was showing that well-being among older adults was related to health *and* the degree of social interaction people experienced.[31] More recent studies demonstrate that involvement of other people in our lives in fact enhances our health and well-being.[32] What the Pennsylvania study and other research indicate is that community engagement and participation not only reduces loneliness, but contributes in significant ways to our health and well-being. Research on the determinants of health shows that social exclusion influences our health status. Social exclusion refers to specific groups being denied the opportunity to participate in community life.[33] Research shows that marginalization and exclusion from mainstream society are key factors leading to adult-onset diabetes and a range of other chronic diseases.

It is not just about the well-being of a vulnerable citizen. It's a two-way street. Participation enhances each person's social network. It's about the well-being of all of us!

Facilitators know the power of community and social inclusion in creating possibilities – for health and participation. It is a two-way street, since participation enhances social networks. It is about the well-being of all of us! More and more, there are stories across Canada of people experiencing community, with all its possibilities and messiness.[34]

What is Community?

There have been many attempts to define community. Some emphasize place and space, some focus on culture and heritage, while others stress common attributes and connections. Still others describe hospitality and relationships.[35] There is a complexity to community that facilitators understand.

As facilitators, we employ a framework that focuses on five inter-related kinds of community:

- Neighbourhood
- Personal networks
- Groups and associations based on common interest
- Third places
- Feelings of connection

Neighbourhood as community. Christie, a young woman, recently moved into a new neighbourhood. The facilitator and Christie asked people in each of their networks who they might know in Christie's new neighbourhood. Christie also told her co-workers about her new neighbourhood. Before long, Christie and the facilitator had identified six people in the new neighbourhood. This created a foundation for Christie and the facilitator to begin a process of building relationships with neighbours.

Neighbourhoods can be a rich resource. Neighbourhoods may be one block on a street, a ten story apartment building, or a six block area. Sometimes, people connect with a neighbourhood that is not where they live. For example, Joe's welcoming neighbourhood is where he shovels snow and cuts grass, even though it is not the neighbourhood where he lives.

When neighbours know each other, natural support usually emerges from the relationships that have been created. Neighbourhood connections can reduce loneliness and isolation. They also create possibilities for shared interests and meaningful relationships. Facilitators know how important it can be for citizens who are vulnerable to be known by others. It is a natural safeguard for others to know you and your routines.

Neighbourhood connections can reduce loneliness and isolation.

Facilitators know they often need to be intentional about how they support someone to be connected with their neighbourhood. Seldom does just living in a neighbourhood naturally lead to relationships and connections. Christie and the facilitator didn't wait around for connections to magically appear – they intentionally created opportunities to meet people in the neighbourhood.

In being intentional, facilitators look for welcoming signs and possibilities that a neighbourhood can, in fact, be a community. We are also aware of the warning signs because this is not always the case.

Personal networks as community. Most people have several personal networks in their lives. Think about the personal networks that you have. You may have a neighbourhood network, a family network, a friendship network, a work related network, and perhaps a network related to a hobby, leisure, or sports activity.

> *The family has thanked me repeatedly now for being persistent in looking at community options for their sister and helping them see and believe in other community possibilities.*

Personal networks are the heart of our lives. They include the people we care about most and the people we do things with on a regular basis. Facilitators understand networks and how enmeshed people are in networks. They help people to identify their personal networks, and to think about how they want to expand or nurture their relationships.

Network development is central work in independent facilitation because it broadens possibilities for community involvements. Facilitators know the networks that exist in their community, and they understand the power of networks as a source of connection and opportunity.

Imagine you are interested in literature – think about all the networks of people in your region that might be interested in literature. Writers, school teachers, librarians, book clubs – many networks share this interest, and once we tap into one network (say, librarians), we are most likely to connect with other people and places that share this common interest. We use networks to expand community and discover possibilities for people to express themselves and their gifts.

Facilitators support people to identify their personal networks, and to think about how they want to expand or nurture their relationships.

Groups and associations based on common interest as community. Community associations refer to the common interest groups that exist in all communities, regardless of size. A town of 4,000 people will typically have more than a hundred community groups and associations – faith groups, service clubs, women's groups,

Facilitators understand the complex fabric of community and see potential and possibility everywhere. We know that the heart of community is about citizenship.

Scout and Guide groups, book clubs, sports groups, and the list goes on. Some are formal groups with a name and structure; others are informal such as the quilting group Aunt Pearl started with a few friends. There are numerous places of common interest for us to become involved, based on our interests and gifts.

Facilitators are aware of the hundreds and thousands of community associations of common interest.

John McKnight has written extensively about community associations: he shows how they contribute to inclusion and citizenship because they are based on trust and participation.[36] When people gather to do weaving together, they trust that each participant shares this interest. Age, ability, socio-economic status, sexual orientation, and skin colour do not matter – what matters is the interest in participating. In associations of common interest, people are members, not clients. John McKnight reminds us that genuine community feels and looks very different from artificial groups congregated by service systems.

Third places as community. Third places are those public spaces where people gather to enjoy the company of fellow citizens. Ray Oldenburg has studied these public spaces and concludes that "third places are great, good places."[37] In third places, citizens can put aside the concerns of daily life and engage with others in conversation. Oldenburg argues from his research that these places – cafés, coffee shops, libraries, bookstores, bars, and hair salons – are essential to a community's well-being and that they contribute to any healthy community.

Facilitators are also aware of the potential of virtual communities. Social networks that are created through Internet, texting, and blogging are part of the lives of people of all ages now. These new resources for communication can be used for expanding community awareness. They will never replace the magic of human to human contact, but can be a catalyst for building connections and conversations.

Facilitators understand the importance of third places and look for ones that are welcoming and that foster conversation and connections. We also recognize that not all third places will be safe and welcoming, and we become astute at knowing the difference.

Feelings of connection. We all know what it feels like to belong, to be part of a community. It may be a family gathering, a self-help meeting, or a spiritual experience with a faith group. Facilitators look for how a person responds to various community settings and notes feelings of connection as a guide. How does this setting feel? Are you comfortable here? Conversations based on questions such as these can enable a

> *Facilitators understand the importance of third places and look for welcoming places that foster conversation and connections.*

person to begin to identify what is working for them in the community. It may also give us clues about what further work may be needed in order to build more welcome settings.

In summary, our sense of community becomes richer and more diverse when we work with multiple, inter-related definitions of community. Facilitators understand and use this layered nature of community and know that community is not just about presence in a place. As Sherri Torgman reminds us, community is also about participation in the "spaces" between the more formal structures of cities and towns.[38] Facilitators search for and discover these hospitable spaces, whether in a neighbourhood, a community centre, a library, a network, or a corner store.

We now know that community engagement and participation is powerful because it expands opportunities. Research shows that success in life depends on the number and quality of opportunities we have.[39] Think about all the opportunities that can be created when we begin to work with community in this way. The astonishing power of independent facilitation also lies in helping others discover this as well. Imagine when a whole group of people believe in community possibilities!

How Facilitators "Know" Community

The five kinds of community assist facilitators and others to think about and experience the complexity of community. Facilitators seek to know the deeper levels of community, and to be responsive to the diversity of people we work with. We become aware of community culture, the meaning of community spaces and places, relationships that enhance community, and how community enables full participation and contribution.

An awareness of *community culture* is an important part of knowing community. What kind of experience does this person have? What cultural experience might reflect their community attitudes and engagement? Facilitators must never underestimate culture and its influence. At a meeting of families interested in individualized funding, two immigrant families from South America recently showed up with six to seven members of each family. The facilitator needed to be aware of the culture of these families' communities and their structure for decision making and participation.

Facilitators understand that knowledge of community places and spaces is also about the meaning of those spaces and places. Community members in the U.K., for example, might not immediately relate to 'neighbourhood,' but they immediately understand 'the pub' as a third place that is like a neighbourhood. We understand the power of place, and also appreciate that places have diverse meanings. For some citizens, the public library is a place to borrow books. For other people, it is a place to go to read newspapers, check email, meet with a literacy tutor, or join a book club.

> *Facilitators are aware of community culture, the meaning of community spaces and places, relationships that enhance community, and how community enables full participation and contribution.*

Facilitators know community through their *broad connections and relationships*. We often have networks which we have nurtured over the years. These can be tapped into to guide others to create or re-build networks and community connections. Consider a local market. On one level, the facilitator knows the main vendors and what is the most appealing food. On another level, we know the best time to go to the market to meet people. We also know which vendors are the most welcoming, and which fellow citizens come to the market on a regular basis. The facilitator sees the potential of the market and other community spaces for connection and relationship building.

Facilitators know community as a place to fully *participate and contribute*. We know that people have a variety of interests and a range of things that are important to them. We also believe that there is a place in community where every interest can be expressed! We are confident that we can find people and places that are interested in whatever someone wants to participate in. This belief in community as a place to fully participate and contribute enables facilitators to see possibilities and to know that they can create possibilities if they do not already exist.

The Role of Community Tools in Facilitation

Facilitators have tools that assist them in helping people to see the potential community offers for participation and relationship building. Good tools serve the facilitator by creating conditions for effective processes, questions, conversation, and reflection.

- **Community mapping** *is a tool for understanding someone's community, connections, and possibilities for community engagement.*

  Community mapping is a process where people are asked to write on a large piece of paper what they are doing in each of the five kinds of community. People are usually surprised to discover that they are more connected in community than they realized. But, it is often the facilitator's questions and reflections that enable people to have this insight. "What routines do you follow regularly?" "What places do you visit repeatedly?" "Who do you know in your neighbourhood?" "Who invites you to do things?" "What other people and places would you like to know in your community?" We do not use tools such as community mapping only with the person we are working with, but also with the people around that person. This creates an understanding of the web of community connections, and often identifies overlapping common interests.

  > *Good tools serve the facilitator by creating conditions for effective processes, questions, conversation, and reflection.*

- **Identifying community assets** *is a tool for understanding the strengths and welcoming places in community.*

  All communities have strengths. Facilitators avoid deficit language and use community assets to build connections and capacity. In exploring neighbourhood, we might ask, "What are the strengths of this neighbourhood?" "Who are the neighbourhood leaders?" In exploring networks, we might reflect on, "What groups of people come together to work on change?" In exploring more formal organizations, we consider, "What are the strengths within this organization?" or "What innovation is happening in this organization?" As facilitators, we use these assets of community to assist us in supporting people to benefit from these strengths.

Strategies for Connecting with Community

Facilitators encourage and support people to create an everyday life by connecting with community life. For facilitators, the process of connecting with community flows from an understanding of people's strengths and dreams.

Judith Snow, a disability rights advocate, says that in some ways, inclusion is like syncopation in music.[40] Syncopation refers to rhythms which are unexpected; they are not routine and often stress a unique beat. Inclusion works, says Snow, when we find the strength that a person brings which was missing before. When we are supporting someone to connect with community life, we are conscious of this person's gifts and how they might enhance a community setting.

When facilitators are supporting someone to connect with community life, they are conscious of this person's gifts and how they might enhance a community setting.

The essence of this part of facilitation is a good process. When a person expresses an interest in a particular goal or hope for their future, the facilitator builds a process that enriches connections to places in the community where that goal will be understood, and perhaps achieved.

There are four ways that facilitators build strategies for enabling people to connect with community:

1. Noticing hospitality

2. Supporting autonomy, meaning and participation

3. Finding connectors

4. Supporting friends/workers to be connectors

1. *Noticing hospitality.*

   Facilitators understand that hospitality exists in various places in community. As David Schultz, a leader in community inclusion, says, hospitality exists "beneath our feet," yet is not always easy to spot.[41] We become adept at noticing potential hospitality. It may be a neighbour that shows an interest. It may be a place where people hang out, such as a café or restaurant. For example, Ahmet has been visiting the same Thai Food restaurant for twenty years and when you see the way he is welcomed and supported, it is no wonder he loves the hospitality and the food! Although finding hospitality is relatively easy when we become intentional in looking for it, we recognize that there are places that simply are not hospitable.

2. *Supporting autonomy, meaning, and participation.*

   Facilitation with vulnerable citizens often needs to explore autonomy, meaning, and participation. As we have noted, many people have not had the opportunity to exercise self-determination or autonomy. People's strengths and hopes for the future often give the facilitator a hint of how autonomy might be exercised. The facilitator becomes skilful at supporting people to express their autonomy in whatever community settings are a good fit.

   Carlee had always loved singing and dancing, and when she expressed the desire to begin dancing again, the facilitator suggested joining The Flow, an informal dance club. She knew the leader was very engaging and would find a way for Carlee to deepen her interest. The facilitator understood that Carlee's desire was not just about singing and dancing but also connecting with others who share her interest. The facilitator notices that others in the dance club benefited from the involvement of a new member and it enriched their experience as well.

3. *Finding connectors in neighbourhoods, community associations, and third places.*

   Facilitators are always looking for natural connectors in community. When Jose wanted to join the local choir, the facilitator connected him with a choir member, who in turn connected Jose with other choir members and helped him to learn the choir routines. Natural connectors are usually people who are good at asking and inviting. Facilitators look for connectors when a vulnerable person requires support to be part of a community association or third place. Connectors can also be found in neighbourhoods.

4. *Supporting support workers and friends to be connectors.*

   Family members, support workers and friends can often be asked, and should be asked, to connect a person with community. This process is often about moving from presence to participation. It involves building confidence in the new connector, who must fundamentally believe that others are likely to be welcoming. They need the confidence to expect a 'yes'. Facilitators get to help build that confidence. They may also be called on to help build the connector's skills. Not everyone finds it easy to make a cold call on behalf of someone else. The facilitator can share concrete tips and strategies and walk with the new connector, who in turn, walks with the person.

In all of these strategies, we remember to stay with the person's aspirations, and notice how they might change over time. In fact, much of the community connecting can shift people's dreams and interests.When people are engaged in community life, they are influenced by their fellow citizens. A web of community relationships begins to form.

A Web of Possibility

When we are connecting someone with community life, we are intentionally building a web of possibility that links a person with neighbourhood, personal networks, communities of common interest, and third places. A web is a powerful metaphor, since it reflects the idea of inter-connected networks and non-linear connections. When we help someone to connect with community, we are assisting them to move from isolation to participation, from exclusion to inclusion, and from presence to participation and contribution. This reflects a variety of connections and relationships that deepen over time and begins to look like a web.

As facilitators, we understand that creating this web requires different approaches for different folks. For some, finding others to make an introduction to new people or places might be enough for connections to take hold. For others, the approach may require extended exploration and experience, as it may take time to become familiar and comfortable with a new setting or new people. Still others may need to develop a trusting relationship with someone in a new place before they become engaged. As facilitators, we invite others to become involved and we look for 'connectors' and introducers in those places.

As we look at the communities of which we are a part, it is very possible that someone invited us to be there. Each of us relies on invitations to broaden our community web. As facilitators we are always supporting others to invite people to join them. It may be a neighbour who also knows some people at our workplace. It may be a family friend who introduces us to a new person, who wants to go dancing. It may be a connection with a community of common interest that leads to even more relationships and possibilities. Sometimes it is a theme that brings people together (healthy eating, book lovers, hiking groups).

We understand that other community members are an important part of the web. Some of these people may need support to be welcoming, to be accommodating, or to become comfortable to invite and introduce others. It may be helping others in a group understand how someone communicates, or how to be helpful.

We also engage others as web builders on behalf of a person. It may be someone such as a family member, support worker, or member of the group who plays the key role in making introductions, or stays with someone while they become comfortable with a new community setting. All neighbourhoods, places, and communities have people who can invite people in, make introductions, and model welcoming and inclusive behaviour. Our role as facilitators is to find them, make links among them and nurture the web!

Community is for Everyone!

Facilitators support individuals to transform their relationships with their community. Many vulnerable citizens are isolated or disconnected from community life. As we get to know people and their longings and hopes for a good life – an everyday life – we consider places that would understand those longings. Inevitably, we will find that almost everyone we work with will desire some form of community. Our role is to support people to move from mere presence in the community to participation and contribution.

Facilitators understand that people are tremendously influenced by the culture of disability, poverty and their previous community experience. Sometimes this means that people will be unfamiliar with, or even be afraid of community. We often need to take time to build a strong, trusting relationship with a person as the basis for building community options. With conversations, coaching, and strong facilitation, people can build an everyday life that is full of relationships and possibilities.

Inevitably, facilitators will find that almost everyone we work with will desire some form of community.

Standing Still to Move Ahead

As facilitators, when we think about community, we often find ourselves feeling a profound sense of connection. As we stand still, we realize that community is where we express ourselves. We come to understand and experience community in many ways. Sometimes we build community, and other times we are lucky enough to stumble into community and are reminded how important it is.

Our most creative work often comes when we are supporting others to connect with their communities. As we stand still, we remember that it is not about finding the perfect or lifelong connection, but instead finding many and varied welcoming places and spaces that make everyday life more interesting.

As you reflect on your community, what connections have you facilitated? What worked well? What parts of community connecting and community building have been challenging for you? What does "embracing the richness of community" mean to you personally? What is most challenging for you? What actions and commitments can you make that will enhance the craft?

Chapter Seven

Making Relationships the Priority

Relationships are central to the New Story and to having an everyday life in the community. Judith Snow, who exemplifies the power of relationships and community, says:

> *All human life is made possible through relationship. Everything we know, everything we choose, everything we learn or do is in some way connected to other human beings. It is not more separateness that leads to vibrant lives of contribution; it is a better quality of relationship and cooperation. Independence does not lead to sovereignty in one's own life — the right sorts of relationship do![42]*

In recent years, research has identified a direct connection between relationships and well-being. We now know that a sense of belonging is as basic a human need as shelter and food. It is foundational to our own sense of well-being, fulfillment, and happiness. It is a key part to living an everyday life. There are well known benefits to inclusion and to having rich and diverse relationships in our lives including an increase in:

> *We now know that a sense of belonging is as basic a human need as shelter and food.*

What Facilitators Know and Help Others To Know

1. Yes, everybody is ready for relationships. It doesn't matter how they communicate or their previous life experiences. Every person is ready to have other people in their lives.
2. Every person has something to contribute to a relationship.
3. People experience community in relationship with others.
4. Isolation should not be an option.
5. There is more than one approach to relationship development.
6. Intentional approaches are usually needed to build authentic relationships.
7. Ask and expect a yes – believe that other members of the community are interested in relationships.
8. Relationships are core to all social interactions: whether one-to-one, in a group, or group to group.
9. This isn't a fad – it's a basic human need.

- Health and well-being
- Social Support
- Safety
- Choices
- Self Esteem & Happiness[43]

Besides research, don't we all know deep down that relationships are important? It is within relationship that we are able to grasp a deeper understanding of ourselves. Our relationships with others can enhance who we are and who we can become. Facilitators in the New Story care about relationships – a lot! The need for relationships is simple and well understood.

The recognition that some of us are disconnected not by choice, but by circumstance, is less understood. Facilitators are likely to witness profound and persistent loneliness. We know and understand that being alone can create another layer of vulnerability. When we recognize the real power of relationships and social networks, we see them as a vehicle to make change in the circumstances a person is facing.

When we recognize the real power of relationships and social networks, we see them as a vehicle to make change in the circumstances a person is now facing.

Relationships also bring security. Having lots of people who know you, and many who love you, means more connections and feelings of security. Many people are clear about what this means to them and to people around them as they age. One mother we know said years after her daughter's circle of friends was well developed, "I can die in peace now and know she will be taken care of." A father we know said about his son's friends, "Having all of you in our lives means there are more eyes and ears watching out for Jeff."

Facilitators think about several aspects of relationships:
- The core aspects of relationship building
- The facilitator's relationship with the person
- The facilitator's relationship with the person's family and friends
- The person's relationship with other members of the community
- The person's relationship to groups of common interest
- A group's relationship to other groups (this is where the community development role of the facilitator comes in!).

Relationships Create Change in Our Thinking and in What We Imagine for Ourselves

Facilitators understand that relationships can be slow to develop and sometimes even harder to maintain. How do we assist people to develop and maintain relationships?

It often begins with listening and respecting.

> *Jay had a history of broken and unsuccessful relationships. He often seemed anxious in the company of others. The facilitator understood that he needed help both to develop and maintain relationships. The facilitator did this in a variety of ways. He tried to model talking to Jay, in the presence of others, in a way that brought out the best in him. Jay happens to be an avid baseball fan and never misses a game on television. They chatted about strategies he could use to reduce his anxiety when in the company of others – excuse yourself to the*

> *washroom for some time to regroup, count to 10 or even 25, put on your biggest smile. As well, the facilitator helped Jay invite people to his own place. Chatting to people where he was most comfortable was just easier for the moment. Over time, as Jay grew more confident in himself and others responded to "the best of him", Jay met more and more people. Over time, he was becoming known and appreciated.*

Another important part of developing and maintaining relationships involves the facilitator paying attention and noticing.

> *Paying attention means noticing things within you and around you. It means showing interest in another person and being aware of their interests and feelings. As people begin to show interest in each other, they begin to engage in each other's worlds. Discovering things in common increases the likelihood of a relationship becoming possible. Sometimes people discover early that there is a certain chemistry that is hard to explain, but we can feel it in our hearts and minds.*

As relationships develop, learning and reciprocity often guide the evolving connection.

> *Think about the close friends you have. There is probably a strong sense of reciprocity. This does not mean equality, but rather involves some give and take. Reciprocity often has to be learned over time – how to nurture a growing relationship, how to build in ways to learn together, and how to find common interests that can deepen over time.*

Facilitators understand that relationships require a degree of comfort and engagement for reciprocity to flourish. This is encouraged and supported in all aspects of our work.

Relationship Development Starts Early

Eleanor is an elderly woman living in a rural area, close to a large city. Her husband died four years ago and she has gradually isolated herself, no longer accepting invitations from other couples with whom she and her husband used to socialize. Her children are grown, with families of their own and live several hours away. She came to Canada from Yugoslavia forty years ago, but still feels her English is poor.

She has spent more and more time watching TV and has worsening health issues.

Eleanor's nurse practitioner has been part of a pilot project to identify the role social networks play in health and well-being. She suggested that Eleanor would be an ideal participant. Eleanor agreed hesitantly.

An independent facilitator was assigned to work with Eleanor to re-establish some social networks and explore other possibilities. The facilitator was much younger than Eleanor and did not have any previous working knowledge of an immigrant's experience moving to North America. She saw her first job as developing a relationship with Eleanor and gaining an understanding of Eleanor's cultural and family heritage.

Eleanor's story illustrates how important it is for the facilitator to begin by forming a relationship. We do not make assumptions about the person because of age, disability, or illness. We begin where a person is, and use our emerging relationship to explore hopes, fears, and possibilities. Even though the facilitator's role was to expand Eleanor's network, she knew that this would not work unless she first had a relationship with her built on respect, trust, and understanding.

> *We begin where the person is, and use our emerging relationship to explore hopes, fears, and possibilities.*

Relationships Include Having More Than One Friend

> **"** *Relationships, relationships, relationships... need I say more?* **"**

When facilitators have a role in assisting others to develop or expand relationships, it is too easy to default to the idea that, if a person has a close friend or an involved family, that's all he or she needs. But facilitators know that relationship development is much richer and certainly more complex than that. We have a broad understanding of what relationships really mean and therefore we know that a range of relationships are needed in order to live full lives. Some relationships are intimate and others are more distant, some people will have a support circle, others will not want that formality – and there is a lot in between! As Aristotle said, "Friendship is a thing most necessary to life, since without friends, no-one would choose to live, though possessed of all other advantages."

We can recognize the benefits of a variety of relationships as well as a large and diverse network. We all know the benefits and positive aspects of having close friends. We also know that there is power in weak, less direct ties, people in our

We all know the benefits and positive aspects of having close friends. We also know that there is power in weak ties, people in our lives who provide us with information, services, and connections.

lives who provide us with information, services, and connections. How many of us have gotten a job because we knew someone who knew someone? This is the power of relationship in claiming an everyday life. Facilitators help others to have positive and supportive relationships with the person. This includes those who love that person, those who know that person, those who acknowledge that person, and those who are aware of that person.

Facilitators recognize that relationships come in a variety of shapes and sizes! Imagine the range of relationships we have in our lives:

- friends of friends

- acquaintances from your fitness group

- neighbours you talk with

- the stranger on the plane beside you

- spouse, lover

- sister, brother, mother, father

- friend since elementary school

- soul mate

- service professionals (the server at Tim Horton's who knows you always order a double double)

- parents of your children's friends

- co-workers

- fellow church or sports club or service club members

The list goes on as we think about who we interact with in a typical day, week, month or season. We see hundreds of people and many of them we get to know very well.

Being in positive and reciprocal relationships expands our way of being and thinking. But equally important is knowing that – both relationships with those who care about us and those where our interactions are essentially commercial – enhance our lives.

You cannot learn to be a friend outside of friendship. You cannot learn social etiquette without practice and social cues found within relationships. And you cannot learn the give and take of conversation without the opportunity to

> *When I first met Marti she was what one would kindly describe as a very exuberant person. She would often start our conversation before I had even emerged from the car. Marti would pull me into the house chatting all the way. It would take some time and some patience for me to have a turn to speak. I hated to admit it, but listening well to what Marti was saying left me feeling exhausted. She flitted from topic to topic and the sheer volume of her voice took its toll. Her mother constantly worried that she was bothering people, thus their isolation was seen a way to protect Marti from disappointment and to protect others from being embarrassed by her.*
>
> *As a facilitator I suspected that Marti simply had no experience in the give and take that occurs in relationships. That she was so hungry for the opportunity to share with another human being, that she got carried away. We needed to get past the fear that isolates her and keeps others from enjoying the energy, enthusiasm of this person named Marti.*

have conversation. It is relationships that anchor us in community life.

> *Eleanor struggled with the facilitator's questions about who she used to enjoy spending time with. After all, those women still had busy lives with their husbands. She didn't want to bother them.*
>
> *The facilitator listened deeply to Eleanor's fears and doubts and gently spoke of how many of those women were likely missing their friendship with Eleanor. Building on how they used to spend time together, the facilitator suggested a reconnection with Hilda, one of Eleanor's closest friends prior to her husband's death. She encouraged Eleanor to call Hilda and suggest a coffee date at the local bakery tea shop.*
>
> *Eleanor tentatively agreed and was pleasantly surprised when Hilda was so warmly welcoming to the reconnection.*
>
> *The facilitator moved at the speed comfortable for Eleanor before suggesting connecting with a few other women she used to know.*

Embracing Social Networks

Facilitators understand the power of social networks. New research is showing how our networks influence us all in significant ways.[44] Think about the friends you have, and the friends of those friends. Think about your family members and connections each of them have. Networks form a web that influences how we think, what jobs we might get, and who we will marry. We are all embedded in networks and they create opportunities for us to find and develop meaningful relationships.

Social networks, in informal ways, are a broad network of friends, acquaintances and near strangers. A social support network is a group of people who you can count on to support you through many different aspects of life. They are the people you can call in good times and bad, to make social plans, just to chat, or to get information about things happening in the neighbourhood and

We are all embedded in networks and they create opportunities for us to find and develop meaningful relationships.

broader community. The frequency with which we connect with those in our social networks is as varied as people themselves.

Most of us have multiple, overlapping networks. We probably have a family network. We may also have a neighbourhood network, a friendship network, a workplace network, a sports or leisure network and maybe even a network of people we see regularly in relation to the predictability of our daily life routines.

One network is not enough. Having six great friends is wonderful, but if they are also the people you live with, work with, and socialize with, it does not enrich your life with new activities and possible new relationships. Particularly if you and the five others are the only ones in their network!

Helping people develop relationships in their community is the greatest legacy we can leave as facilitators. Having many strong relationships ensures long-term security and well-being. As Pat Worth, co-founder of People First of Ontario, said, "Services can't love me, as well meaning as it is. Only people can love me."[45] Similarly, one of the characters in William Paul Young's book, *The Shack,* says, "It is true that relationships are a whole lot messier than rules, but rules will never give you answers to the deep questions of the heart and they will never love you."[46]

> *Helping people develop relationships in their community is the greatest legacy we can leave as facilitators.*

Margaret Wheatley, a writer studying organizational behaviour and leadership says,

> *Despite current ads and slogans, the world doesn't change one person at a time. It changes when networks of relationships form among people who share a common cause and vision of what's possible. This is good news for those of us intent on creating a positive future. Rather than worry about critical mass, our work is to foster critical connections. We don't need to convince large numbers of people to change; instead, we need to connect with kindred spirits. Through these relationships, we will develop the new knowledge, practices, courage and commitment that lead to broad-based change.*[47]

Facilitators help others to be aware of and understand how social inclusion and social exclusion influence the relationships we have and often the behaviours we exhibit. We will often hear that a person's behaviour is the reason for his or her isolation. As facilitators we ask if isolation is the reason for a particular behaviour. The two are often entwined.

We rely on our social networks for:

Strength. As the saying goes, "We are stronger together."

Variety. Our lives are enriched by the role models and people in our social network. Often, members of our social networks are varied in their interests, talents and gifts. These are shared freely and the exchange makes our lives more interesting.

Shared Understanding. Members of a network may find others who share common situations. These groups can be very supportive and safe places in which to try ideas, learn together, mentor and support one another.

Information. Networks are an incredible source of information. If you want to know about something, having a broad range of people to ask is useful.

More Invitations. Members of our networks often invite us to meet and become engaged with others they know.

Support. Having a close knit group often anchors us as we explore community, create our own identity, and take risks. This type of core group coming together is often referred to as a support circle.

> *Eleanor was feeling more confident now that she was spending time with Hilda once a week or so for tea. And she had seen a few other women at other times on the street and actually stopped to talk — something she hadn't done for several years.*
>
> *Hilda invited Eleanor to join her for lunch with a new friend. Again, Eleanor was tentative about expanding her connections, but the facilitator encouraged this 'sharing' from Hilda's network. Eleanor felt Hilda might be feeling sorry for her and extended the invitation for that reason. The facilitator talked with Eleanor about how this sharing of people from each other's network happens all the time in everyone's*

life and helped remind her of how she used to do just that when a new family would move into her own neighbourhood.

When they did have lunch together Eleanor was invited by the new woman to take part in a knitters group that was teaching youngsters at a local school how to knit. Eleanor thought of her own granddaughter, living so far away, and thought she would very much enjoy working with children.

The facilitator also had noticed that Eleanor spent a lot of time talking about her husband. She missed him a great deal. The facilitator suggested joining a women's grief group. Eleanor was against the idea, feeling that her English would be a barrier and feeling she would be out of place. The facilitator talked to Eleanor about the importance of living outside of assumptions about herself: an older immigrant woman with poor English. Eleanor did agree to have the facilitator make a call to the group leader to talk about possibilities. The facilitator called and explained Eleanor's hesitancy. The leader offered to phone Eleanor personally to try to increase her comfort level with coming to a group. Eleanor was open to receiving a call, but wasn't making any promises to go to the group.

Facilitators Nurture Relationships in Wider Community

Theodore Roosevelt said, "The single most important ingredient in the formula of success is knowing how to get along with people." Facilitators understand this in our own lives by constantly nurturing our own connections and relationships in the wider community. We know how valuable it is to know (and get along with) a range of people in our community. When we have a relationship with someone, they will more likely trust us or take time to hear our request. If we know someone who knows the person we are trying to meet, we create a path for easier access. Our community connections and relationships help us to access the resources we might need as part of our facilitation. Our relationships in the wider community enrich the lives of people we support.

There are many ways that facilitators intentionally build relationships in the wider community.

- Being aware of nurturing and learning from our personal networks.

  Charlene has an active social life. As a new facilitator, she began to notice how her networks work. Her book club, for example, includes several women who are very involved in the arts. She realized that she had learned a lot from these women and noted that she would be able to call on them in the future when she was exploring issues in the arts with people she supported.

- Noticing hospitable people in a range of local places and spaces.

  Charlene also began to notice the hospitable places and spaces in her community. She realized that she had known several shop keepers for years and had very positive relationships with them. As a former recreation worker, she also had very strong relationships with workers in two community centres. She began to think about how these relationships could be helpful in her facilitation work.

  Our community connections and relationships help us to access the resources we might need as part of our facilitation. Our relationships in the wider community enrich the lives of people we support.

- Keeping a journal about key people and places.

  With the encouragement of her facilitation coach, Charlene began to keep a journal. At the end of each day, or sometimes at lunch hour, she noted her feelings and thoughts about her facilitation. An important part of this recording was to list emerging relationships and connections that she thought might be valuable to nurture. Charlene has deepened her awareness of her community relationships as a result of her journaling.

- Mapping our own relationships.

  Charlene and her fellow facilitators spent part of a day exploring relationships. As part of this work, each facilitator created a map of their relationships. Charlene's map was quite rich with relationships, but she noticed that she had few connections with neighbours. She decided she had better work on her own neighbourhood relationships to enhance her life, learning, and connections.

- Asking and inviting.

> *There were several people in the community that Charlene wanted to meet. All were people she felt she could learn from, who could be like mentors to her. One was a professor who did research on community development. Another was an artist who had written a book on creativity. A third had created a project to help homeless people find affordable housing. She asked each of these people if she could have coffee and conversation with them. She was delighted to discover that everyone was more than willing to meet. She learned so much from each person she met, including how readily others will share their own relationships and connections. Charlene has decided that as part of her work she will meet one new person in her community per month.*

Role of Facilitators in Making Relationships the Priority

For many facilitators, helping others to develop a range of relationships leading to varied personal networks is a natural fit. Other facilitators will have to depend on their courage, vision, passion, and principles in order to carry out this work. Sometimes it takes a lot of time, work, and intention to build ordinary relationships.

Facilitators meet many people who have an over-reliance on one or two family members, often parents, to meet their social needs. Families have often taken on this role, but it is not enough. The presence of an independent facilitator, in fact, allows parents to be family members again, while the facilitator takes on the role that many families assumed was theirs.

> *The presence of a facilitator, in fact, allows parents to be family members again, while the facilitator takes on the role that many families assumed was theirs to hold.*

> 66 *A young woman, Sabrina, was living on her own for the first time. She was having difficulty eating in a healthy way, despite repeated attempts by her mother to get Sabrina to 'eat properly.' After lots of conversation, Sabrina and I decided to create a healthy eating group. We invited several of her friends to join the group, and five of them responded enthusiastically. The group now meets every 6-8 weeks with a different theme each time (such as 'creative veggie dishes'). Each person brings a dish as well as a recipe to hand out. Sometimes we role play after dinner and we always have great food and lots of laughs. These five women get along so well now and you can tell that they really look forward to these evenings. Sabrina is now beginning to eat better and has deepened her relationships with five friends.* 99

We know that relationship development is intentional work. The pervasiveness of loneliness tells us that relationships do not just happen. We need to always introduce, invite, entice, and connect people. Finding or creating places and spaces for hospitality to flourish is often the beginning of relationship building. We will find ourselves helping others to find common interests, place of mutual comfortableness, and connection. Sometimes as facilitators we act like social secretaries. Our role is helping people become aware of each other but also encouraging them to make commitments (meet at the movies, share dinner, ride together to an event). All of this serves to bring people together in ways that they can come to know and appreciate each other.

In the book *Friends & Inclusion: Five Approaches to Building Relationships*, facilitators are always looking at their work through a relationship lens.[48] This relationship lens gives us a way to look at the world and to begin to fully explore this idea of relationships with others. We facilitators are, in many ways, like a broken record always asking "who?" Who knows this person and can help bring out his or her gifts? Who knows someone who knows someone who might like to meet this person? Who has a connection that will help this person expand their imagination?

As a strategy, facilitators also use people's desire for self-improvement as a way to discover and engage others and to build relationships that will begin to address the issue. Again, we do not just ask 'what' can we do, we ask 'who' can we ask to assist us with this issue.

We have a facilitator friend who is well known for the Who question. She is a true connector. One night she called a fellow facilitator whispering on her cell phone from a washroom in a local restaurant.

> *"It's me, Marilyn. I am so mad. I am at the restaurant with Jim and the hairdresser I met through you. They are getting along great. I can tell they really like each other."*
>
> *"So… why are you mad?"*
>
> *"They are having so much fun that they want to order dessert. You know I gave dessert up as my New Year's resolution. But if I say no to dessert, they might end the evening without making other plans. So I am breaking my resolution and it is only January 5th!"*

Yes, we facilitators are a conniving bunch. And sometimes we just have to eat dessert. It is a small price to pay for the sheer joy of connecting people with each other.

Facilitators may also notice that the greatest opposition to developing a broad network of relationships are sometimes those closest to the person at the centre of the process. Families often resist the idea out of love, and fear of the rejection their family member may experience. They may fear abuse or exploitation. Addressing this may be a large part of the facilitator role: helping people take the risk needed to build relationships in order that the person they care about can experience belonging, connectedness, security, and joy that will come to enrich his or her life.

Yes, Everyone is Ready for Relationships

Relationship development should be considered a transforming aspect of the work of independent facilitators. Seeding and supporting positive relationship development is a vital part of our work.

There are strategies that help with relationship development. These are questions that facilitators rely upon.

1. **Naming.** Identifying relationships that a person has is often a first step to change. What relationships past and present can this person depend upon? If the answer is none, then we must begin. If there is one, then how can we help this person to fully engage as a friend and who else does that friend know who can be engaged?

> " *We can get overwhelmed when we think about people with disabilities and their desire to belong. It does not have to be that way. We have to get started. Introducing people to others, one person at a time, means the journey has begun. If you never begin then people will never belong.* "

2. **Inviting.** As we invite people to share in the lives of others, surprising things happen. As facilitators we expect a yes. Who can I bring? Who can you bring? Who has met someone who would enjoy meeting this person? And we also encourage and support others to do the inviting.

3. **Connecting.** Think about common interests and community associations. What are the spaces and places where relationships have a chance to germinate and grow? As people gain experience with each other, the vulnerable person has an opportunity to enhance their valued roles in the community.

4. **Sharing.** If we think about it, many of our relationships have been borrowed from the networks of other people. We all share our relationships. Some of us even share family. When we introduce a new person to people we know well, we have just shared our network. Also, it is not unusual for different networks to overlap, so that some of my friends are part of your network.

5. **Support Circles.** Support circles bring a formality and intention to relationship development. It is a place to begin, but it is certainly not the end of relationship development. In fact, identified support circles members can also have a primary role in helping a person have a broader and more diverse network on which they can depend.

As facilitators we know that we often are invited to meet and share people in one another's networks. Imagine if the members of an intentional support circle saw themselves as inviters, connectors, and introducers. And, in turn, they supported those they introduced to also do the same. Over time, the support circle would no longer look like a closed circle with predictable roles, but instead it would become one piece of an intricate and complex web of relationships. Not everyone we come to know is part of our support, but support circles become part of everyone we know. Support circles ask this question frequently, "Who knows someone who knows someone who might like to meet the person we have come to love?"

The Role of Relationship Tools in Facilitation

Facilitators also have more formal tools that can help them structure their work to help others become focused on relationships and their benefits. These tools offer us a chance to hone our questions, create a visual record, note progress, and understand our own interconnectedness.

- **Relationship mapping** is a tool for understanding one's own network of family, friends, and acquaintances — it also helps us to identify the potential to develop, expand, and nurture more relationships. Relationship mapping is a process where people are asked to write down who they have in their lives — friends, family, workplace colleagues, members of schools, faith communities, neighbours, etc. People are often

> *An important role I have as a facilitator is to assist people to build circles of support. This is an intentional invitation of people the person has chosen to support them. I usually help people to see that the circle can be about friendship or support, or both. A circle does not include all members of the person's network, but consists of people that the person trusts to assist with decision making. Often I help people create circles during crises, when someone needs advocacy or direct support during a difficult time or transition. I also strongly support the idea of forming circles when someone in a person's network recognizes the value of bringing people together to be intentional about supporting the person to create a good life. There is no magic formula about how or when this should happen. I love the power of circles as a way to enhance someone's relationships. The networks of each circle member become a rich source for borrowing relationships and deepening connections.*

surprised at the number of people in their lives. Relationship mapping is enhanced when we ask not just the focus person, but also others in the person's life to be engaged in the process as well. Relationship building begins the moment we intentionally decide to connect with someone.

- *Asking New Story questions* of ourselves and others as a tool for understanding gaps, lack of opportunity, and for moving towards a future of seeking possibility for new and meaningful relationships. Facilitators come to know that their work in network development is often a question of Who?

  - Who loves this person?

  - Who can I bring?

  - Who supports this person's family?

  - Who can act as a champion for this person?

  - Who can help this person enhance their identity and reputation?

  - Who enjoys the same things as this person?

  - Who has a network this person can share?

  - Who is sharing places with this person now?

  - How can we support this person to be more engaged with family, friends, acquaintances?

  - Who has met someone, who knows someone who might want to meet this person?

Eleanor found she was getting busy again. She was thinking less about her health issues and more about the things she needed and wanted to do each day. Hilda became a close friend and even offered to go to the women's grief group with her the first time.

The knitters group also became a strong network for Eleanor. She was part of the group that advocated with the school board to make the teaching of knitting part of their existing inter-generational program. Eleanor could hardly believe she agreed to be one of the speakers at the Board of Education meeting but she did know that having a friend sitting beside her made it possible!

Through the intentional work of the facilitator, some of it gently encouraging and some of it making direct contact to explore possibilities, Eleanor began to build her life again through relationships and an expanding social network.

Tough Spots in Relationship Development

Connecting a person to another person or group has its challenges. Some of those challenges may be within the person themselves or with their family. Sometimes the community context is an impediment to relationship development. At times, the challenges will be within us as facilitators.

We know that the majority of people do not want to sit home watching TV by themselves day in and day out. We cannot count the number of times in our work as facilitators we have heard statements such as "James likes his own company, he is happiest when he is watching TV." Oh really?! This kind of statement raises a few questions. What experience has James had with people? What makes aloneness preferable? What experience and information would it take to change that? What are the other barriers to James participating in his community, and what supports might change the situation? We ask questions that encourage reflection and self-awareness.

People often need support to connect with their community. Facilitators cannot have this connecting role long-term. However, we keep the idea alive. We model the ways in which it is possible to connect people to each other. This is what engages others in the process. We know it takes others in a person's life to intentionally develop, nurture, support, and expand relationships. It is the only thing that really matters. It is the foundation on which community life is built.

> *We ask questions that encourage reflection and self-awareness.*

The Power of Relationships

Facilitators work from a relationship lens, noticing possibilities for networks and friendships. Sometimes these possibilities are close to home. We notice how family relationships might be strengthened, or how connections in the neighbourhood can be deepened.

We learn as facilitators that our understanding of community is deepened when we intentionally work with a relationship lens.

Sometimes relationship possibilities exist further from home. As we get to know a person's strengths, we find ways to connect those skills, interests, talents and gifts with others who would understand them. We see possibilities in the myriad of groups that exist to share common interest. These places become fertile ground for relationship building. We learn as facilitators that our understanding of community is deepened when we intentionally work with a relationship lens.

As facilitators engaged in independent facilitation, we understand that social networks are a powerful way to produce change in the world – sometimes one email can link people quickly around an issue of concern. We know that networks work and we see it often – an idea is generated and before long, lots of people embrace the idea.

We role model the ways in which it is possible to connect people to each other. This is what engages others in the process.

It may be a healthy eating group, a neighbourhood gathering, a common interest we share with others. We support people to understand their networks and we encourage the development of support networks and circles that walk with people in the community. We know there are numerous ways for people to connect and we know that having relationships can make an incredible difference in building an everyday life.

Standing Still to Move Ahead

What do we mean when we say relationships are the priority? As we stand still, we realize that none of our work is possible without relationships. We cannot assist another person to build an everyday life unless we form some kind of relationship with them and they in turn form relationships with others. Our work begins with this relationship, and then builds over time with a range of relationships, all for the purpose of assisting people to pursue what is important to them.

As we stand still, we become aware of the skills we need to develop relationships. We need to notice and act upon possibilities for relationship development. We need to take time to nurture our own relationships and learn from that process for our facilitation. We need to be aware of strategies for relationship development.

What have you noticed about your own networks and relationships and how they might inform your facilitation? What are you seeking on behalf of others and are you willing to ask for it? What skills of relationship development do you need to make a commitment to work on?

Chapter Eight

Holding the Process of Person-Directed Planning

There is growing recognition that good planning is a powerful tool for producing desirable outcomes. Planning is no longer about just finding support funding or plugging someone into a bed, placement, or service. It is about helping people define and create an everyday life for themselves. As facilitators working in the New Story, we know that good planning is also more than a checklist that gets covered in one annual meeting, which is what is often seen in a systems approach to planning that requires little facilitation. Service plans are rarely rooted in community, relationships, or self-determination.

Good planning is a process of engagement that provides a way of discovering:

- how a person wants to live his or her life

- what is required to make that possible

- who can support this process along the way.[49]

Good planning is a process of engagement.

In essence, we now know that good planning, accompanied by clear action,

> **❝** *Formal personal planning is only one of the many roles (functions) a facilitator has. It is natural to plan – it happens for all of us – minute to minute, day to day, year to year. It is important that as facilitators we hold dear this idea of natural planning and only formalize that which is a struggle, needs a nudge, or input from others. Planning is not a way to create a new schedule of activities but instead highlights where we can find belonging in community as well as enjoyment and support in relationships.* **❞**

results in a better quality of life while at the same time being cost effective. This has been confirmed in research for people with disabilities, aging adults, their families and support systems.[50]

Earlier, we spoke of the role of facilitators to help people weave a life of meaning, participation, contribution, and relationship by working with individuals, families, services, and communities. One of the tools we use is planning.

Planning is a collective effort centred on a person, often with the support of his or her family and network. Participation is expected from everybody. Facilitators guide the learning, experience, and action needed for a person to plan for, and engage in, a fully inclusive life in their community. The person at the centre of the planning process is the decision maker. The person makes decisions about all aspects of their own life: who they want to spend time with, what they want to do and how they will do it based on the discovery of their own interests, skills, talents, gifts, and dreams.

Planning is a process that may lead to a document (sometimes called a plan), but good planning always leads to action.

What an incredible opportunity we have as facilitators! We create the environment

The facilitator ensures all the pieces of dreams, relationships, self-determination and community are kept alive during the planning process.

to gather all the pieces together — dreams, aspirations, relationships, self-determination, and community — into a process that can truly reflect the person engaged in the planning process. Again, we are responsible for and hold the process by being aware of everything going on and actively employing the values, knowledge and skills needed in each particular situation.

We also pay attention to building capacity with others to ensure that planning leads to shared action. Part of the framework for the facilitator is the mindful use of values, knowledge, and skills to ensure that the planning process is truly directed by the person.

Facilitators are building the capacity of people and their networks to direct their own planning processes.

When the planning process is designed to be a process in self-determination, with the goal of creating social relationships and building capacity, over time the confidence and competence of people and their networks grow. 'Over time' is an important qualification; planning is not a one-time event, but happens over time as people and their networks gain confidence in planning and moving to action. We are in it for the long haul – deepening our relationships over time with the person and their family and friends (networks). In this way, we are building the capacity of people and their networks to direct their own planning processes.

Planning in the New Story is person-directed planning. Person-directed planning that is authentically driven by the person requires some fundamental changes in thinking, in assumptions, and in practice. Independent facilitators know that person-directed planning also requires a shift in the established balances of power. This intentional power shift will occur as we support people to direct their own lives in collaboration with family and friends.

The Emergence of Planning

Historically, well-intentioned services in the disability sector have been all things to a person: residential providers, personal support, companionship, specialized services, and recreation and leisure providers. In other sectors, such as poverty initiatives, services often only focus on solutions, not the cause of a person's struggle. People's lives have

66 *I felt as though I had a licence to create. I had never truly worked for an individual and family without being bound or restricted by policies, bureaucracies, or the influence of others within an organization. As an independent facilitator, I was able to test, challenge and experiment, absolutely nothing was ruled out. I had the space, encouragement and freedom to create and to co-create with that person!* 99

often been predetermined by the services offered rather than based on their individual needs or aspirations. And while services may be based in community, people's lives are often not. Criticism of these service-driven approaches led to person-centred thinking.

The history of person-centred planning goes back to the early 1980s when Jack Yates developed the Individual Service Design. In the 80s and 90s we saw the development of other person-centred planning tools: Personal Futures Planning, MAPS and Circles, Essential Lifestyle Planning, Frameworks, PATH, and Recovery Planning.

In the mental health field, Mark Ragins developed the Four Stages of Recovery, a framework designed to help people with mental health issues achieve their goals for life in the community.[51] Ragins identifies four concepts – hope, empowerment, self-responsibility, and a meaningful role in life. The role of self-determination in planning your future is critical to both recovery from a mental health issue and to building a meaningful life. In the developmental disabilities field, person-directed planning and facilitation grew in concert with the move to individualized funding.[52] Increasingly, provincial governments are emphasizing person-directed planning in policy and legislation.[53]

In the New Story, independent facilitation is valued as a way to ensure that supports and services meet individual needs and aspirations. Facilitators independent of services and funding bodies are free to create a collaborative process that is truly reflective of the people and the direction they decide on.

When Planning is Especially Useful

Being intentional about planning can give direction and purpose to life. As the Cheshire Cat in Alice in Wonderland said, "If you don't know where you are going, any road will get you there."

There are a number of reasons that an individual or family might choose to involve an independent facilitator in a person-directed planning process. In the book *Creating a Good Life in Community: A Guide on Person-Directed Planning*, five reasons are identified:[54]

- Things are changing (e.g. life is in a transition stage, like leaving school or moving away from your parents' home).

- Self-Determination (e.g. all people want choice and control over their lives).

- Having Community Options (e.g. when discovering that the community is full of things to do, places to go, and people to meet).

- Solving Problems (e.g. problems can be easier to solve when you share them with others and have others to help you).

- Directing Supports (e.g. figuring out how to direct the people who provide support to you).

Planning with an independent facilitator may also be useful for:

- Crisis planning (e.g. helping set a path for a shorter period of time for someone in distress).

- Recovery planning (e.g. helping people identify what they need to recover from mental illness or addiction).

- Health planning (e.g. helping people with new health challenges map out their choices/actions around their health).

Facilitators know when planning might be appropriate. We also understand when the planning process might need to move to action fairly quickly, or when planning can be more reflective and exploratory. For example, a family in distress may need immediate, supportive action as part of their plan. On the other hand, a young person beginning to plan the transition to life after high school may benefit from a planning process that takes place over months or even years.

Guidelines for Person-Directed Planning

Whatever the vulnerability of the person whom the facilitator is assisting, guidelines for person-directed planning provide direction for the process. These guidelines highlight the broader New Story principles, but also reflect the work of facilitation. Facilitators want to be sure that any plans that get developed fully honour the people and their wishes.

Guidelines for Person-Directed Planning

- Values the person's voice first, often with support and input from family, friends and networks. The person directs the planning process.

- Allows for many ways to communicate, recognizing that people have a variety of ways to tell us what they need and want.

- Is different for each person. Although there are guiding values and doctrines, there is not a single planning 'format' that must be followed.

- Is part of an ongoing facilitation process that recognizes people's changing lives and needs.

- Reflects the person's skills, interests, gifts, and longings.

- Discovers and builds on the person's strengths, abilities and capacity.

- Acknowledges that each person has a unique history of experiences and this is part of who they are.

- Helps people have meaningful experiences and build capacity of their community and all it has to offer.

- Is intentional about assisting people to build, nurture and sustain reciprocal relationships.

- Develops a shared understanding of all the possibilities for a better future.

- Creates opportunities for everyone involved to be engaged in a creative process with the person.

- Always leads to deliberate action by having clear expectations of what will happen, by when, and who will support the action. Obstacles are identified and steps to overcome them acted upon.

- Explores resources in the community as a first resort. Community is where people will find much of want they want and need in life.

- Creates opportunity for the person to think about "prevention" as well as solutions for "crisis" and places high value on investment support.

- Develops safeguards that work well for the person.

- Maximizes opportunities for community inclusion, contribution and participation in valued social roles.

- Informs services about the amount and type of support that makes sense. This enables the services to design individualized, responsive and reflective services and supports.

- Provides information so service providers can create an individualized budget.

- Is an ongoing process that builds in time for reflection, evaluation, and more planning.

- Creates support for negotiation, mediation, and contract development.[55]

Facilitators Hold the Planning Process –
But Not the Decision Making

Facilitators always design the planning process with a person and in collaboration with others identified by that person. We would never begin without the person participating in the process to the best of his or her ability. Perhaps eventually the person will lead part or all of the process. Or perhaps not. We are always aware that we hold the process, but it is ultimately directed by the person. In our society people often want quick results. Facilitators stay with the process and pose questions and design conversations so that people can make their own decisions. This usually takes more time. This idea of holding the process rather than directing it can be challenging but over time, it becomes more comfortable.

> *Facilitators are always aware that we hold the process, but it is ultimately directed by the person.*

- *Carol has been a facilitator for many years and regularly helps people living on the street get the supports they need to create a new life. It is important to her to spend as much time as possible with each person over a period of time before starting to help them create a plan of action. She spends time with people in the places where they are comfortable sharing their thoughts and feelings – and that is most often in abandoned houses, and in parks. Even when she is concerned about their health and safety, she does not suggest moving faster if the person is not ready. That is hard for Carol, but she recognizes that if the person is not in control of his or her own planning process, it would just be another disempowering experience.*

- *Sarah was quite worried that the people she invited to help her think about her future would say she wasn't ready for a job. She and the facilitator agreed on a silent signal to use if Sarah became overwhelmed in the get-together and wanted to end it. It was in fact used when one person expressed strong feelings about Sarah's inability to handle employment situations. Sarah had the control to end what she felt*

Facilitation Reflection on Planning Process

Purpose: *To reflect on the planning process as facilitators*

1. Overarching questions to guide this reflection
   a. What went well?
   b. What could have been stronger?
   c. What did I learn?
   d. What informs good practice for the future?
   e. What would I do differently another time?

2. Setting up the process. I have…
   a. ensured that there has been time to get to know the person/family
   b. developed a clear purpose with people – why are we engaged in this planning process?
   c. created hospitality, so people are comfortable with planning collaboratively
   d. respected and recognized the person as the decision maker

3. Facilitating the process. I am…
   a. being guided by New Story principles
   b. aware of and demonstrating in my work that this is a strength-based process
   c. using planning tools that make sense to the person and situation
   d. creating space for conversation
   e. identifying action steps
   f. building experience and capacity for the individual, family, self

4. Overall reflection. I am intentional in my work and can identify…
   a. what is building
   b. what is missing
   c. what different approaches might be helpful
   d. who is supporting the person with the action steps/decision making
   e. what individuals and groups may be helpful and supportive

5. Taking care of myself as a facilitator, I can identify…
   a. what is supporting me in this process with this person
   b. who is supporting and nurturing in this work
   c. what other learning I may need.

This facilitation reflection is used by facilitators working with Facile Perth County as a guide for their work when holding the planning process with an individual or family.

was negativity. The facilitator noted the comments of the person and ended the meeting. Sarah and the facilitator then met to talk about next steps. Sarah was the decision maker about the planning process.

- *Nathan had no experience in directing his own life. As the facilitator and Nathan got to know each other, it became clear that Nathan trusted a few people in his life but wasn't really comfortable when they were all together in a meeting. The facilitator helped Nathan create a recipe card to mail to people asking on one side what they felt Nathan wanted in his life and on the other side what they wanted for Nathan. The cards were sent with a self-addressed stamped envelope. When they came back in the mail, Nathan and the facilitator went through the cards and captured the main ideas. Nathan then was able to choose which ideas he wanted in his action plan.*

The Facilitator Guides the Questions

As we live our lives, many of us often take time to ponder and reflect on what we want or need. We may not gather people we love and trust together in one room, but we often check in with our family and friends about things we are thinking about for our future.

> *Planning often needs to be an intentional process... ultimately it is about creating an everyday life.*

This is one way of planning – reflecting, informally getting feedback, and then charting a course of action. Although we may not think consciously about how people we trust impact our decisions, our planning is rarely done in isolation.

Planning often needs to be an intentional process that helps people to pause and consider what changes are needed, what could be better, or what experiences could enrich life. Ultimately it is about creating an everyday life in which the phone rings often, and people have meaning in their daily activities.

In this planning process, there are many questions to be explored. However, instead of actually asking a series or prescribed list of direct questions, facilitators use the questions to construct conversations. As explored in Chapter 3, asking open-ended questions designed to create dialogue is an important part of our role.

Planning is an ongoing process, not a one-time meeting, so the conversations are also ongoing.

Important Conversations

Relationships. Facilitators need to gain a sense of a person's relationships, past and present. This gives us a picture of the person's personal network. There may be people who want to help the person plan their future. There may have been a former pastor who really connected with the individual. There may be people who have come and gone. The conversations are more than a listing of who the person currently spends time with. We look deeply in these conversations for possibilities of *who*: who might be currently involved in helping the person plan; who might be an emotional support; who might help the person find a job; who cares but doesn't know how to help.

Decision making. Facilitators ensure a supportive decision-making process is in place. This is true even if the person cannot communicate in a way that is clearly understood. This requires intentional conversations about how people will listen. What does the person want for him or herself and how do we know it? What do others want for the person? What is the common understanding of a supportive decision-making process? For example, a facilitator working with Carrie, a young woman, might have a series of questions. Does Uncle Bob think it means that Carrie can't make her own decisions when she is struggling with her mental health? Does Carrie's best friend think it means Carrie should never be told to go to the hospital no matter what danger she is to herself or others? Carrie's facilitator would help Carrie have these conversations before, during and after any difficult times. For someone who does not use language at all it brings a different set of questions to create the conversations.

Imaginations and Longings. We are fortunate as facilitators to be welcomed into people's imaginations and longings. It is an honour to notice people discovering what fills their hearts with joy. There are also struggles in the planning process, in helping people to imagine a better future and to help it become reality. Past hurts, lack of experience, a disbelief in a better life, can all limit someone's vision. Facilitators create conversations that go beyond what vacation someone wants to take next year. We ask probing questions, not just of the person at the centre of the process, but also of those around him or her, to spark dreams and longings to emerge, or to consider possibilities for action. People who do not have a clear sense of their future can more often identify what they do not want. That is often the starting point for the conversations.

Strengths and Interests. What is the most dreaded question in a job interview? *What are your strengths?* It is human nature (or at least Canadian nature!) to be hesitant to talk about what we're good at: our skills, interests, talents and gifts. It's much easier to identify it in others – facilitators have the happy task of creating those conversations.

Needs. We all need things in order to function effectively in our daily lives. Facilitators don't shy away from this. Discovering someone's needs is part of creating a whole picture. It helps the person's network and future service providers give the best support possible in the best possible way. We frame needs as routines or requirements, not as deficits. Needs simply are part of who we are as humans. However, facilitators must notice and listen for any negativity that creeps in while discussing needs.

Community Opportunities. Facilitators craft conversations, reflecting a person's relationships, longings, strengths, interests and needs, to lead everyone to see community as a first resort for possibilities. We ask where the person's gifts will be welcomed in their community, where a need can be met, where relationships can be developed. We understand the power of place. We support people to find places where their longings and strengths will be nurtured and amplified.

Capturing the Plan Through a Written Document

Written plans will be as diverse as the people who make them.

There are many different planning tools. Facilitators select their tools carefully and do so in order to help someone deepen their understanding and awareness. Facilitators need to avoid an over-reliance on planning tools. Which tool we use doesn't matter as much as the values and guidelines we adhere to in the process. It is quite probable that the best planning tools are a good ear, blank paper, a clear purpose, the right questions, and a gathering of the right people.

Often it is important to pull all the information together in one place. This can be called the person's personal plan, and is generally a written document. Conversations about what this could look like include questions about the purpose of the document, how the person will be clearly heard, what directions need to be identified, how it will be used, implemented, and monitored. How will it be kept alive and not forgotten on a shelf? Facilitators make sure there has been dialogue about any need for a written plan.

The person decides who else they would like to be part of the planning process.

Written plans will be as diverse as the people who make them. We bring ideas to the person and his or her network about what might be included in a written document.

What is the purpose of the plan?

Facilitators know there is power in having a clear purpose. There must be a clear reason for developing a written plan. The purpose then guides the planning process. We may be assisting people and their networks to build a plan that also meets formal system requirements, such as funding or direction of supports for service. Or the plan may be designed to assist with a transition, a crisis, or specific health needs.

How will the person's voice be heard in the document?

Can it be written by the person? Can poetry, pictures, scans of their handwriting, or quotes from the person be used to ensure their voice is heard? Can the person determine the look and feel of the document? Does the plan avoid jargon and human service lingo? Is it easy and inviting to read? Does it reflect the culture of the person? Does it make you feel like you have met the person even if you have not? Voice is also reflected in the goals and directions; are they truly owned by the person?

> *Not every plan needs to include every aspect of a person's life.*

Who else is part of the planning process?

The person decides who else he or she would like to be part of the planning process. We make sure that any written plan clearly distinguishes what is important to the person from what is important to all of the other people in that person's life. (i.e. It is clear which statements are from the person and which are from others?)

We also make sure a person's privacy is respected by identifying who needs what information from the plan. Some plans may clearly say who cannot have access to information in the plan (e.g. private information is kept in a brown envelope with a note on the front about who has access).

What gets written down?

Not every plan needs to include every aspect of a person's life. All written documents are different, but may include an outline of strengths, hopes, goals or directions, and action plans. The way the document looks and feels will vary. For example, Karen, the yoga teacher, had a plan with various yoga poses guiding each section. Gerry, the musician, had various musical notes as his headings. Barb, the poet, had poems throughout her plan.

Are goals clear?

Facilitators capture what a person and network develop as goals for the plan. These emerge from conversations about relationships, dreams, longings, strengths, interests, needs and community opportunities. They may only come one at a time, but we recognize and capture them. The goals *must* reflect what the person wants to move toward. Research on goals is clear – they will not be effective unless they are authentic and meaningful to the person.[56]

Are actions clear?

The facilitator also ensures that the plan identifies who is responsible for implementing action items. In the plan, various network planning group members will take on responsibility, as will community partners. And there may be roles for paid service providers.

Who will monitor and review?

Another critical part of any plan is clearly defined responsibilities for monitoring to ensure it is being implemented in the way it was set out. This includes ensuring that people at the centre of the plan have the opportunity to build the skills and knowledge to effectively monitor their own plans. This monitoring function helps ensure that the written plan is a living document. In this sense, the plan should reflect changes that have occurred as well as noting emerging opportunities.

Dealing with Conflicting Thoughts

The person is the focus of the planning process. The facilitator believes in the right of people to be their own decision makers, and also in their capacity and potential capacity. At the same time, we understand that we must listen to many different perspectives in the planning process if we are to create a rich, meaningful process.

> *The facilitator believes in the right of the person to be their own decision maker, but also in their capacity and potential capacity.*

A challenging part of our job is helping to ensure a productive process when confronted with contradictory thoughts and ideas. Sometimes differing ideas emerge from the people who have gathered to help the person think about the future. Facilitators need to help everyone see the commonalities, focus on the person, and make room for differences. Sometimes the best we can do is help the group come to a place of respectful disagreement. In a supportive decision-making situation, where the person is not able to articulate clearly what he or she wants, this place of disagreement is rife with potential hazards. If it is not clear to the person's network what the required action is, then less effective action will follow. Facilitators note and name differences, but make sure people do not get stuck in them. Our work is to find common ground and to do what is necessary to keep the group moving forward in ways that benefit that person.

These issues of honouring differences and finding common ground are very real for facilitators. Conflict may be between a person and their parents, or between a person and a service provider. We often have to juggle, and yes still hold, a process that respects everyone at the table. Ultimately, there are times we, using the skills of listening, creating conversations, and negotiating, must help the person and/or network come to a decision.

Planning is One Aspect of Facilitation

Facilitators working in the New Story can master a technical planning style, but more than anything we need to grasp the heart and soul of the process. This calls for us to be reflective in our planning and facilitation work. We need to be mindful, listen from the heart, and create questions for deep conversations. We need to believe that as people have positive experiences on which to build, it is likely that the unexpected will happen.

Facilitators understand that planning is really about assisting people to create the change needed to claim an everyday life rich in relationships and contributions. For people who have little experience with self-determination, planning is designed to give them voice and control over the issues that matter to them. Planning might also involve family and neighbourhood. It might mean assisting a family with summer planning to ensure that their children are well supported in the off-school times. Other

> *The ways we plan are endless, but we know that planning weaves in and out of the process of facilitation.*

times, we might assist a neighbourhood to share gifts so that everyone has more hospitality and possibilities for participation and sharing. The ways we plan are endless, but we know planning weaves in and out of the process of facilitation.

Standing Still to Move Ahead

Our understanding of planning has been shifting. The emergence of 'person-directed planning' implies that a person directs his or her own future. As we stand still, we recognize how profound this notion is in reality. It also signifies a shift in the culture toward recognizing that all people can participate in their own life journey. Planning has traditionally been about 'a plan' that would somehow direct what people did for the person.

As we stand still, we recognize three significant shifts in our thinking about planning as facilitators. First, we see planning as only a part of the facilitation process. The intention of planning implies a promise to take action. Second, we embrace the planning process with its various conversations, approaches, techniques, and decision making as fundamentally more important than the plan itself. Third, we accept planning as a dynamic process that requires us to fully engage in listening, creative thinking, and relationship building. People change and create multiple paths over time, and we learn to adapt with them.

What have you noticed about how planning in this way has impacted your work as a facilitator? What is most comfortable for you? What are the limitations of the planning tools or processes you may be using? What is important for you to practice in order to enhance your facilitator craft?

Chapter Nine

Safeguarding Everyday Lives

Facilitators recognize the importance of safety and security for people who feel they are at risk in their community. Building safeguards into a plan or process with people is sometimes even more important to the people who love them.

Safeguards are intentional actions taken to reduce known or perceived risks. When built from the New Story principles, safeguards are a positive way to achieve a sense of security and well-being in community. Helen Keller said, "Security is mostly a superstition. It does not exist in nature. Nor do the children of men as a whole experience it. Avoiding danger is no safer in the long run than outright exposure. The fearful are caught as often as the bold. Life is either a daring adventure or nothing." This challenging quote from Helen Keller means that we need to balance dignity of risk with security. To focus on the latter by itself is to miss the point of building everyday lives in the community.

We all have safeguards in place as we live our lives, whether we have particular vulnerabilities or not. Vulnerability is not a reason to be excluded from community life, nor is it a reason to fear it. As many women living in urban areas will tell you, they are aware of the risks of living in the city but are not prevented from everyday life because of them. It does not mean that women are not cautious or aware, but it does mean that they balance perceived risk and actual risk with safeguards, such as parking their car under lights at night, or not walking alone through isolated areas.

There are a number of factors that contribute to a person's vulnerability. Any of us may experience these at various points in our lives, but many citizens live with them their entire lives, making vulnerability a chronic condition. This includes being poor, lacking relationships, being unemployed, having poor health, and lacking a social safety network.[57]

Sheila Mansell, a registered psychologist from Calgary, provides us with some insights into the reasons adults with disabilities are more likely to be at a heightened risk of vulnerability:

- socialization practices that promote and reward compliance and obedience
- limited access to relationships and friendships
- limited opportunities for social engagement
- limited knowledge about body and sexuality
- limited experience with, or success using assertiveness
- receiving intimate care and services in isolated settings.[58]

It is reasonable to apply some of these insights about people with disabilities to other people who face similar environmental limitations.

Safeguards may be a way to make us feel more comfortable with risk. It is sometimes easy to get carried away by what could go wrong. Facilitators also help people get carried away by what could go right when the appropriate personal safeguards are in place. Orville Endicott, a well-respected legal counsel, suggests that laws don't protect people; instead, people protect people and laws sometimes help people to protect people.[58]

> *Safeguarding is one of the things that makes facilitation truly transformational.*

In some ways, safeguarding is one of the things that makes facilitation truly transformational. Life is often a fragile balance between risk, safety, and security. By being intentional about building positive safeguards, we help people build lifelong support in their community.

Ways We Safeguard Our Lives

There are several ways that citizens safeguard their lives:

Having people who know us well
Facilitators assist people to find and nurture relationships that are lasting, durable, supportive, and reciprocal. This includes family and friends as well as co-workers and neighbours. *This is the power of close ties.*

Having people who barely know us
Facilitators also recognize the importance of having people who barely know us, but know our routines, such as the woman who serves our coffee every morning at the coffee shop. These people would notice us missing if we didn't show up. We help people recognize that regular participation in community is a safeguard. *This is the power of weak ties.*

Having a purpose in life
Facilitators help people to discover what gives meaning to their day. Having a reason to get out of bed every day, contribute, and participate in what is happening around us, leads to more routines and connections. *This is the power of purpose.*

Having an identity in community
Facilitators assist people to know who they are both in spite of and because of their personal challenges. Discovering how we can identify ourselves and be identified under different labels – artist, yoga teacher, social networker, advocate, worker, musician, volunteer, or friend — provides a social status. Having status can be a protection against manipulation or exploitation. *This is the power of valued roles.*

Having confidence and competence
Facilitators assist people to build skills, confidence, and competence. This includes the skill of recognizing when someone is trying to take advantage. Knowing your rights is also an important part of having confidence. *This is the power of being aware of our own rights in relationship with others.*

Telling our story

Facilitators assist people to tell their stories. Sharing stories changes the way people think about who we are, what we can become, what we should expect. As importantly, stories change community. Sharing our gifts with neighbours through our story can change attitudes and perceptions. *This is the power of sharing in community.*

Formal safeguards

Laws, policies, and regulations that address discrimination and exploitation are important safeguards we have agreed to as a society. Other formal safeguards include guaranteed income for those who cannot work and landlord/tenant acts that ensure housing is safe. *This is the power of societal expectations.*

> " *I have found it so important to keep myself grounded in good principles when facing a situation that involves safety. It's too easy to default to protecting someone at all costs rather than figuring out how they can be not only in control, but also safe.* "

False Safeguards

We can learn from our own history. At one time as a society we invested heavily in what we now know are false safeguards. We have learned that the institutionalization of people does not safeguard them, and in many instances has caused irreparable harm.

We also know that funding alone does not safeguard people. Bricks and mortar, no matter how modern or how beautiful, do not safeguard people. A mindset that perceives difference as a reason to segregate and isolate members of our society does not safeguard them. Despite the best intentions, facilitators can find themselves still influenced by our history when people act in ways that are unfamiliar or unpredictable. Facilitators need to be aware of our tendency to revert back to false safeguards under the guise of protecting people.

While we want to be sure to be doing "due diligence," we also must be careful to whenever possible maintain individual's rights and freedoms.

It will be a delicate balance to look at these issues and possible improvements and yet ensure we are not violating these inherent rights and respect afforded to all citizens in our society. One does not want to cross the line into being overbearing or 'big brotherish' in the attempt to provide protection.[60]

Facilitation and Safeguards

As facilitators, we are aware of the tension between risk and security. This tension can play out in a variety of ways. It is often related to people's hesitancy to embrace social inclusion. How would this person manage in an inclusive setting? Would she be accepted by others? We work with these kinds of questions, and help people understand

Facilitators need to be aware of our tendency to revert back to false safeguards under the guise of protecting people.

the dignity of risk and the ways we enable people to feel safe and secure. Facilitators work toward building confidence and competence in the people we support. In part, this might involve showing how everyday life can change for the person and still be safe. We identify various types of safeguards and how they work together to create a holistic approach to change.

When developing strategies about informal safeguards, facilitators recognize that in order to change thinking we must change the questions people are asking. We shift from "What places can keep this person safe?" to questions such as "What gives each of us a sense of security as we participate in community life?" We often need to explore these questions gently with people over time.

Facilitators build understanding about safeguards without people falling into false traps and without creating angst and concern. We need to help others think about this in a way that upholds a commitment to self-determination, relationships, and community.

The safeguard framework provides a lens through which facilitators notice possible issues and places where people may need support.

Simon Duffy and John Gillespe, social innovators from the U.K., help us look at safeguards in this way:

Self-determination. I am at greater risk of abuse if I cannot direct my life, if I cannot communicate and if I am not listened to.

Direction. I am at greater risk of abuse if my life does not suit my preferences or character and if I am perceived by others as lacking social value.

Money. I am at greater risk of abuse if I lack money or if I cannot control my own money.

Home. I am at greater risk of abuse if I cannot control who I live with, who comes into my home and if I cannot protect my privacy.

Support. I am at greater risk of abuse if I have no one to help me and if I cannot control who helps me.

Community Life. I am at greater risk of abuse if I am not part of my community, if people do not know me and I have no chance to contribute to it.

Rights. I am at greater risk of abuse if there is no publicly understood and enforced protection for me from the abuse of my rights.[64]

Relationships and Networks: Facilitators know relationships and networks are crucial. Supportive relationships which are enduring and dependable over time can reduce vulnerability. Both formal support networks, such as Support Circles, and broader informal networks have an important role in solving problems, dealing with adversity, supporting our resiliency, and helping us grow in our self-determination and self-control.[62] These relationships can provide both practical support and emotional security.

> *It is absolutely critical that informal safety nets also be considered, as when the rubber hits the road it is often these informal networks of friends, family, neighbours, and community members that provide the real safety net for individuals, as is the case with all of us.*[63]

Facilitators know that having a well-established community presence that includes predictable routines increases the number of people who recognize us and expect us at a particular location. Having established valued roles on which others depend not only increases our self-identity but also increases the number of people who depend on us and on whom we can

As facilitators, this means ensuring that no one travels through community unknown or alone. We all need the eyes and ears of others.

depend. Over time a person will have more positive experiences on which to build a successful and supported life. This often means sharing the importance of being in the community, and being seen in the community. This may be something that is not valued by people. Facilitators keep this at the forefront. We cannot be recognized if we are not present regularly.

Decision Making: Facilitators have a role in assisting the person, his or her family, and network to acknowledge that each of us want to fully realize ourselves as a decision-makers in our own lives. Of course, our vulnerabilities may require us to rely on others to guide and support us. Regardless, the decisions have to be what makes sense for us and our lives, not always what makes life easier for those around us. Any interventions deemed necessary for purposes of safety are revisited frequently and only used when necessary. We need to figure out how to have ongoing opportunities to learn, practice and grow in our ability to make good decisions and build on the success of our experience. We often learn good decision-making skills by doing. Having people who can support our decisions is often necessary. Being trusted to do what is best for oneself builds confidence. As facilitators, this means we must maintain an ongoing focus on the importance of who ultimately makes decisions.

Technology: As technology becomes more accessible, facilitators look for more and more ways to use it in order to reduce a sense of vulnerability and increase safeguards. Technology can be used to both enhance independence and connectedness. From cell phones and talking calendars to the GPS, the possibilities of matching the right technology with a person are seemingly many. As a facilitator this means introducing these ideas to individuals and those around them so they can consider their potential benefits and ways that technology can enhance a sense of security.[64] This can be life-changing.

Financial Security: Conversations about financial security often emerge during the facilitation process. Possible sources of income may include employment, self-employment, parental contribution, Registered Disability Savings Plans, Henson Trusts, and trusteeships. Discovering ways a person can move towards financial security is often extremely important to parents concerned about their own aging and the security of their loved one. There may also be discussions about Power of Attorney and signing authority on bank accounts. As a facilitator, it is critical that we bring the principles of self-determination to the financial discussions to increase the opportunity for people to have control over their own finances. When people need support with handling their money, the facilitator asks questions that help them arrive at arrangements that provide that help while encouraging them to be as engaged as possible in decisions about their money.

Balancing Risk and Safeguards

We can choose to let fear guide our lives and lifestyles, or we can be secure in believing that community safeguards can be trusted.

It is easy to perceive greater risk than actually exists in community. We need to be cautious in our thinking about safeguards. It is easy to be led by our own preconceived notions about what is possible or impossible for others. Some people are particularly vulnerable to this judgemental thinking. The following chart shows how a person, with the support of a facilitator, explored questions that led to community participation.

Asking Questions That Lead to the Least Restrictive Safeguards

What do I want?	*Is there a perceived risk or an actual risk?*	*What are the possible safeguards for me?*	*What safeguard options make sense to pursue?*
To go to the movies by myself.	Taking the bus home at 9:30 at night. Walking from the bus stop to home. Being alone on the streets at night – possible robbery or assault.	Have a cell phone and know how to call 911. Call my parents when leaving the movie and when arriving home. Invite a neighbour to go to the movies with me.	Right now, I need to do all three things. But within a month I want to feel okay with just having my cell phone.

Negotiating Safeguards with Alex

Alex is a young man with a disability who wants to have money in his pocket in case the guys at work go for a beer at the end of the day. It is important to Alex and his co-workers that he can participate in this sort of activity, so they can all feel part of the team. His mother is reluctant because Alex has been known on more than one occasion to give away all his money when asked to hand it over by a gang of troublemakers downtown. Of course, it is not a good thing for Alex to be losing his money. But it is also not a good thing for him to miss out on the camaraderie among his co-workers or for his life be guided by his mother's fear of Alex being taken advantage of.

As facilitators it was our role to help Alex and his mom explore the idea of safeguards. We asked questions that led to conversations about what enables Alex to be spontaneous in his relationship with his co-workers while at the same time being less vulnerable as a target for his cash, and how Alex can have more control over his finances. We also explored what experience his mother needs in order to trust and support the rather ordinary decisions Alex is making for himself.

As we explored this we learned some things about Alex's current situation:

- When Alex said he had no money, the gang left him alone. He was not at risk of physical harm. When Alex carried money he was always honest in his response to the gang.

- Alex has a limited understanding of the value of money but his spending patterns are quite predictable.

- Alex has a good relationship with the people at the bank where he goes every Friday to withdraw his money for the week.

- He gets his money in five-dollar bills and he now carries no more than two five-dollar bills in his pocket.

- Alex uses his pocket money to pay for his coffee at break time.

- If he wants to make other purchases, his mother or support worker always carry his money and make the purchases for him.

In this instance, the facilitator led a few minutes of brainstorming with Alex and his mother, which brought about some possible creative solutions. Alex can role play saying "no" when people ask him for money. He can carry a bank card for an account that has small amounts of money in it for infrequent and unexpected expenses. Alex can take a different route to and from work so he does not have to interact with the troublemakers. He can see if there is a co-worker who wants to share rides in exchange for some gas money. Any one of these options is a possibility. Alex and his mom agreed to try those that bring them the greatest sense of security.

Out of the above conversation other worries began to emerge and over time provided opportunity to further explore safeguards, while at the same time enhancing self-determination, relationship development, and community participation.

Alex's mom was worried that his co-workers may drink too much and not be able to give him a ride home, and that she wouldn't be able to remember all his comings and goings with this new routine. Alex was unhappy at the idea of his mom asking too many questions when he did get home. His mom was worried that if she didn't ask questions then she would be unable to find out if he was being taken advantage of.

This time the facilitator assisted Alex and his mom to have a number of conversations, and encouraged them to allow for some low risk trial and error. Over time they were both able to feel comfortable with the following safeguards:

- Alex carries a cell phone with the numbers for his mom, sister and neighbour pre-programmed.

- Alex leaves information about his expected daily happenings on his talking calendar for his mom to listen to if she forgets what is happening that day.

- Alex agrees to trust his mom and come directly home when she helps him understand that she is getting agitated.

- Alex and his sister chat by phone regularly instead of his mom asking all those questions when he gets home.

In this story, it was the role of the facilitator to guide conversations and help Alex negotiate safeguards. It is in this way that Alex and his mom could begin to distinguish between what is imminently dangerous and what just causes a sense of discomfort, and all the variables between. We understand that fear cannot dictate people's lives. It cannot be an excuse for disallowing people to express themselves. It cannot be a reason for prolonged social isolation.

However, we do recognize that the idea of safety, as well as intentionally thinking and building safeguards that balance the risks of community life with our desire to belong, participate, and contribute, can be freeing and liberating. As facilitators we are building the capacity of others to think about safeguards in a measured and rational way.

When Safeguards Go Too Far

We know that being aware of safeguards within a facilitation process is a good thing. We also know that all of us organize our lives so we maximize our sense of security and personal well-being. However, safeguards cannot become the dominant player in the room. How do we know when we have paid too much attention to safeguards in our work as facilitators?

Facilitators are aware of safeguards, but focus our conversations on the positive aspects of living in the community when issues of security arise. We have to think about safeguards as a way of enabling us to get on with our lives, not as a reason to prevent living. There is always risk in living and this has to be acknowledged, and then we have to move on ...toward everyday life.

When Safeguards Are Working

How will we know if safeguards are working? We will know safeguards are working when people feel safe and secure, when people have choice and control over their own lives, and when other people understand the importance of self-determination, community, and relationships. We will know safeguards are working when people have the support they need in times of transition and times of stress, and when we can count on other members of our communities to be aware, supportive and responsive to neighbours, co-workers, friends, and strangers. When people have others they can count on to keep information that is important, that provides a degree of security. This makes us all safer. As facilitators, safeguarding lives means supporting people to become aware of their own voice, to connect with valued places in the community, to deepen relationships, and to create everyday lives. As we strengthen safeguards in this New Story way, we are building the capacity of people and communities.

> *As facilitators, safeguarding lives means supporting people to become aware of their own voice, to connect with valued places in the community, to deepen relationships and to create everyday lives.*

Standing Still to Move Ahead

Helping people think about safeguarding everyday lives is part of our work as facilitators. Because of the deeply personal and relationship-oriented nature of our work, we recognize that people hold us in great trust. Paying attention to safeguards deepens the trust that others have in us. People know that we take the craft seriously, and that we pay attention to the little things that sustain and protect everyday lives.

As we stand still, we come to understand that safeguarding is built on the foundation of our craft - principles, relationships, and community. Living the principles with integrity enables us to 'stay the course' with people even when we, as facilitators, face tough spots. Relationships are so central to safeguards, as we have repeated over and over. Relationships address the loneliness and isolation that so many people experience. Community life in all its richness and messiness also has an enormous safeguarding quality. We help others understand there is a risk to health and well-being when a person is segregated or isolated from the community.

What safeguards have you identified in your own life? What insights does this give you about safeguarding the everyday lives of others? What areas of safeguarding do you need to learn most about?

Chapter Ten

Standing Still to Move Ahead

In all the training that facilitators may receive, little attention is usually paid to self-reflection. But it has an enormous impact on how well we do our work. As Francis Bacon said, "In contemplation, if we begin with certainties we shall end in doubts; but if we are content to begin with doubts, we shall end in certainties." Ultimately self-reflection is about honing our craft.

We have built in self-reflection throughout this book. Standing Still to Move Ahead, at the end of each chapter, has been an opportunity for you to reflect on the craft of facilitation. Self-reflection has been the motivation for us to embark on writing this book. A Sufi tale says that you teach what you need to know. As authors, we believe this to be true – certainly for us throughout the journey of creating this book! We see ourselves as lifelong learners and yearn to further define, and yes, even shape the craft of independent facilitation in a New Story as it is emerging in Canada.

We believe strongly that we cannot continue to learn and move ahead if we do not reflect on where we've been and how we've been there. Some self-reflection can be shared with fellow facilitators, and some self-reflection should, indeed, be kept to oneself. As facilitators in a New Story, how can we possibly discover what strengths and gifts we personally bring to this work without pausing and reflecting? Similarly, how can we learn from our struggles without reflection? An unexamined facilitation career can lead to becoming stuck in a rut and no longer enjoying our work! Times change, perspectives change, and *we* must change in order to adapt and remain relevant in the ever-changing world of facilitating everyday lives.

> " *I couldn't possibly feel I was doing my job if I didn't stop every now and then and ask myself what I could do better. I see it as an obligation I have to the people I work for — and to myself.* "

As facilitators we've probably all left a meeting with an "I nailed that one!" feeling. We've also probably all left a meeting with a "What in the world happened?" feeling. The ups and downs of our work can be hard on us personally. It calls for personal reflection: what did I do that helped it go well? What did I do that contributed to it going off the rails? How can I process that dilemma and then let it go?

In the work we do, we are often so focused on process with others that we may forget to stop and recognize our own piece of the story. If we truly believe we are all in this together, we must then have a key role in the story. It is a piece that is not told publicly — in fact it is rightfully, intentionally omitted in stories about the successes of people who have changed their lives in the community. Yet we need to know and understand our part in the stories, so that we can continue to learn and grow over time, just as the people we walk with on their journeys.

It is a Personal Journey

People reflect in different ways. For some, journaling about experiences, thoughts, and feelings works well. For others it may be conversations with others and thinking out loud with a trusted confidante that brings insight. For still others it may be a meditation practice that allows deeper contemplation.

We need to know and understand our part in the stories, so that we can continue to learn and grow over time, just as the people we walk with on their journeys.

Whatever the approach to self-reflection, there are some questions we can ask to learn more about ourselves. Reflecting is not just about what might have gone wrong in a situation, it is also a way to further understand our skills and our contributions. It is about intentionally keeping good practices and distancing or discarding poor habits. It is a way to deepen our craft as facilitators and become more mindful human beings.

Questioning Ourselves

Besides reflecting on core skills, there are questions we should ask about personal style.

- What is my 'style' – how does my style impact the process and outcomes for people I work for?

- What are my personality tendencies that can help/hinder my facilitation?

> 66 *Over the years I've done a lot of reflecting. The insights I've had have helped me be a better facilitator. I know how important anchors are in my life, like my family. This has helped me notice what anchors are important to other people. I can then help them identify what they need.* 99

In reflection we will find that we are naturally good at some skills. This may cause us to become over-reliant on a smaller set of skills than what is required of us. As we reflect we will want to think of skills and tools that we want to learn or become better at using over time.

Some Tough Questions for Myself

- Where have I failed as a facilitator in the past?

- Where have I succeeded?

- What have I done well and how can I make it a habit?

- What principles am I comfortable with?

- What can I do to be more proactive in my professional development?

- What do I find most meaningful in my work – when and where does it happen most?

- What resistance do I need to address in order to move forward more optimistically and with a fresh mind?

- What types of situations do I tend to ignore or do I need to spend more time with?

- How do people react to me and what do I think that means?

- Which tools do I continue to use out of habit or laziness?

- Are there any aspects of independent facilitation that I am ignoring out of fear of change or lack of knowledge? (e.g. technology)

It can be difficult to identify our positive contributions. Spend time reflecting on your strengths and gifts. Celebrate that you are an important piece of the puzzle as well.

It can be even more challenging to face our own shortcomings. John O'Brien, a well-known educator and author, says, "You know you are making progress when you meet resistance. You know you are making the most progress when you meet resistance in yourself." Honestly acknowledging our limitations is easier said than done. Even more difficult is accepting them and figuring out what is needed to improve and move on.

Of course, once we identify areas we need to work on, the logical next question is, what am I going to do about it? The important step is to take our answers to our self-reflection and turn them into positive, resolute statements that give us concrete goals on which to focus.

Making Time for Reflection

It is about intentionally keeping good practices and distancing or discarding poor habits. It is a way to deepen our craft as facilitators and about becoming more mindful human beings.

Whether it is journaling, meditating, or conversation, making time to stand still for reflection isn't easy. We must be intentional in building it into our work. Some facilitators take a few minutes after each engagement to write in their journal. One facilitator we know uses a recorder to capture her reflections. It doesn't matter where you self-reflect, only that you do it earnestly, energetically, and mindfully.

Journaling

As facilitators in the New Story, we find journaling a very useful tool for reflection. Journaling has two inter-related purposes: to provide space for personal reflection and learning, and to provide a record of the progress of our work.

A personal reflection can capture feelings about the facilitation experience:

"I felt sad and glad at the same time. I could see the pain in the family, but I also saw their exhilaration and resilience! I think I have to make sure I stay centred and not be reactive… their energy is magnificent and I know I really need to respect that and bring balance too. Will have to think more about my role in that…"

A record of progress might capture an event including process and/or outcomes.

"This fifth network meeting had good energy and purpose. The group was very focused and paid a lot of attention to Bob. Their listening has deepened and there is a great understanding of the process. Three network members (Mary, Joe, and Tanya) all spent time with Bob since the last meeting and all were genuinely pleased with their growing relationships. Bob told a story about going to the hockey game with Joe and how they met a co-worker and his wife (Dan and Lucy)."

"Our intentional focus on building relationships in community seems to be paying off, although I continue to spend a lot of time with Bob and his mother to make this happen. I am wondering if I need to re-engage his brother and the pastor, since they were instrumental when Bob left school, but have not been involved with the network in the last two years."

It is a Journey with Other Facilitators

Facilitators, regardless of their level of experience, will want to know who they can turn to for guidance and direction and shared reflection.

Avoid working in isolation! How can we be creative and inspired and keep up our skills without colleagues to share our experiences and ideas? Connecting with other facilitators gives energy to our personal journey. "Who can I connect with?" is a vital question we need to ask ourselves as facilitators.

Connecting with others doing New Story independent facilitation helps deepen our craft as facilitators. We can build strong communities of practice. Across Canada and the United States, facilitator networks are emerging as a key part of the New Story.

Facilitators, regardless of their level of experience, will want to turn to others for guidance and direction and shared reflection! It is an opportunity for:

- Self-discovery – deepening our own knowledge and skills.
- Mutual support – supporting each other to work through tough spots.
- Shared learning – learning and growing individually and together in our work.

" *I don't know what I would have done if I hadn't had Lou (a fellow facilitator) to talk to during my involvement with one particular family. Their family culture challenged me and I found myself struggling internally with respecting their decisions. Lou was a sounding board for me – it saved me!* "

Sometimes we find that guidance from a more experienced facilitator in our own community is most helpful. If you are a facilitator in an independent facilitation organization, you may have the benefit of ongoing mentoring and coaching. Some of you may have to discover an experienced mentor or coach in a different community. As a Buddhist proverb says, "When the student is ready, the teacher will appear."

Mentoring and Coaching Helps Facilitators Grow

It has only been in recent years that the idea of mentoring and coaching has taken hold as a way to strengthen those practicing the craft of New Story facilitation. Both mentoring and coaching are built on the values of self-reflection and collaboration.

The words 'coaching' and 'mentoring' are often used together although they mean very different things.

Coaching tends to be very specific, time-limited, and goal-oriented. Coaching helps facilitators strengthen their abilities to use particular skills in appropriate ways. The coach provides opportunity to practice facilitation skills and review is built into the time together. By focusing on the facilitator's skills, coaching provides feedback in ways that lead to improvement.

Mentoring tends to encourage an intentional and longer-term relationship. Mentors help facilitators identify issues, develop insights, and support creative solutions that are unique to that person. The mentoring process encourages facilitators to use and expand on the facilitation skills they already have. Mentoring is very focused on helping a facilitator to, notice themselves and reflect on that. Mentoring enables experienced facilitators to share their craft with those with less experience. More experienced facilitators can also mentor each other. In this way, facilitators can then create strong networks of practice that provide mutual support.

Experience has led us to believe that the best way to root newly acquired facilitation skills and give energy to well-used tools is by offering a well-developed approach to mentoring, coaching, and practice.

Facilitation Leadership Group, 2010.

It is a Journey with Community

One of the most important aspects of self-reflection is the commitment to broaden our insights beyond our working world. Do we connect with others outside the field we are working in to deepen our understanding of the work of facilitation? Do we read and review research beyond our current work environment?

We often begin this journey with the question, who else in my community would understand this work? What might I gain by connecting with them? Can I deepen my insights about social change in collaboration with others and bring those lessons back into the world where I facilitate?

We may gain a whole new perspective of collaboration or community development

We may gain a whole new perspective of collaboration or community development or planning tools by connecting with facilitators from other fields.

or planning tools by connecting with facilitators from other fields. For example, if I work in poverty initiatives, it might mean exploring how facilitators are working in developmental services. It is particularly helpful in reminding us that most issues are not specific to the people we are working with. In other words, most issues that people face are truly community-wide issues.

Accessibility is an example. Lack of accessible curbs may be an issue for people with disabilities in a community. But it is also an issue for seniors and parents with strollers. Accessibility needs to be seen from a broader community perspective. Once we discover this, it opens up a whole new way of facilitating change; we can mobilize people in a community to advocate for accessible curbs rather than help one person with a disability that we're involved with learn a new route to work that avoids bad curbs.

In the communities in which we work, we participate in a range of networks. These networks, while typically informal, connect us with a range of people and places in our community. These networks enable us as facilitators to know the assets of our community. Consider how these connections deepen our facilitation work – connections with the local market, the community centre, the arts community, the neighbourhood association, the women's institute, the school council, the regional library, and the local volunteer centre, to name a few.

Building the New Story in our communities will be enhanced when independent facilitation is grounded in sound principles and ongoing reflection. As facilitators, we understand the need to 'stand still' and constantly reflect on our personal journey. The independent facilitation organizations that are emerging across North America also need to build in reflection with their facilitators and others. This intentional work honours what the science of motivation is teaching us, that autonomy, mastery, and purpose give people meaning and engagement.[65] Independent facilitation entities create a container for facilitators to work in very meaningful ways with their craft.

The insights in this book calls for each of us to notice within ourselves which pieces of the craft we do well and which need further development. We built reflection questions into each chapter for you to have that opportunity as well. We discovered new things about ourselves through this process of standing still to move ahead. We hope you are able to do this on your learning journey, and that you find it as rewarding as we have.

Acknowledgements

This book has its roots in our New Story work in several communities. We are very grateful to colleagues who have walked with us to help create communities that include all citizens. A heartfelt thanks goes in particular to the pioneers from Perth County and Waterloo Region in southern Ontario who have had the foresight to embrace the New Story with all its possibilities and challenges. Special thanks is also extended to the hundreds of people who have taken our facilitation training courses through the Facilitation Leadership Group (www.facilitationleadership.com). Your questions, feedback, and insights have proven to be invaluable to our own learning.

Several dedicated friends and colleagues reviewed earlier drafts of the book and to them we owe our great appreciation. The feedback and insights were immensely helpful. Thanks to Rhonda Alcott, Laura Armstrong, D'Arcy Farlow, Peggy Hutchison, Theron Kramer, Melanie Panitch, and Cathy Smith. A very special thanks to David DeVidi, whose editing of later drafts was nothing short of exquisite. And a note of gratitude to Wade Sanford who was there with IT support in moments of panic.

Although we take responsibility for the final manuscript, we could not have completed this challenging writing without the support of reviewers and our families.

About the Authors

John Lord is a facilitator, researcher and author who lives in Kitchener-Waterloo, Ontario. John was a founder of the Centre for Community Based Research and its first director for more than a decade. He is also the founding partner of the Facilitation Leadership Group, and is involved in training and supporting the development of independent facilitation. John has published widely on innovative community supports, and has been a leader for the development of what he calls a New Story. John's seminal book on the New Story was published with his wife and long-time collaborator, Peggy Hutchison. Now in its second edition, *Pathways to Inclusion: Building a New Story with People and Communities* is widely used across Canada in colleges and universities. John is also the author or co-author of several other books, including *Shifting the Paradigm in Community Mental Health, Impact: Changing the Way We View Disability*, and *Friends and Inclusion*.

Barbara Leavitt's experience includes extensive development and delivery of value-based workshops and training sessions with her company, lpw associates (www.lpwassociates.com). She has also been involved in the development, implementation and coordination of individualized funding and a brokerage system of support; agency evaluation; helping people and their families plan; helping people develop relationships and circles; and working with people to form self-advocacy groups. She is the co-author of several books, including *Her Shoes Are Brown, Jumping the Gap*, and *Voices: Speaking out on everything from education to discrimination*. Barbara is an Associate with Facilitation Leadership Group.

Charlotte Dingwall is a facilitator and author. She has developed training in the areas of value-based planning, inclusion, and circle of supports. Charlotte has worked as a trainer and mentor to both new and seasoned facilitators, she has collaborated extensively with communities developing options for citizens. She has also worked with many communities over the years on their learning journey towards independent facilitation. Charlotte is a co-founder of the Facilitation Leadership Group (www.facilitationleadership.com) and author and co-author of several books, including *Kirby's Lane: A Well Travelled Path* and *Creating a Good Life in Community: A Guide to Person-Directed Planning*.

END NOTES

1   For an analysis of some of the 'rotten outcomes' of conventional human services, see E. Schorr, *Within Our Reach: Breaking the Cycle of Disadvantage*. New York, NY: Anchor Press Doubleday, 1988.

2   See John Lord and Peggy Hutchison, *Pathways to Inclusion: Building a New Story with People and Communities*. Concord. ON: Captus Press, Second Edition, 2011.

3   Lord and Hutchison, *Pathways to Inclusion*

4   Quoted in Direct Payments Report, United Kingdom, 2003 (author unknown).

5   Paulo Freire, *Pedagogy of the Oppressed*. New York: Continuum, 1970

6   For an exploration of metaphors for facilitation, see Christine Hogan, *Understanding Facilitation: Theory and Principles*. London: Kogan Page, 2002.

7   Paul Born, *Community Conversations: Mobilizing the Ideas, Skills, and Passions of Community Organizations, Governments, Businesses, and People*. Toronto: BPS Books, 2008.

8   Paul Born, pp. 9-73

9   For a thorough exploration of questions, see Michael Quinn Patton, *Qualitative Evaluation and Research Methods,* Third Edition, (Chapter 7 on Interviewing) Newbury Park, CA: Sage Publications, 1995

10   Bob Williams quoted by Tom Nerney, Richard F. Crowley, with Bruce Kappel: *An Affirmation of Community; A Revolution of Vision And Goals: Creating a Community to Support All People Including Those With Disabilities*. The Center for Self-Determination, 1998.

11   Patricia E. Deegan, Recovery and the Conspiracy of Hope. Presented at: The Sixth Annual Mental Health Services Conference of Australia and New Zealand, 1996.

12   Doorway Project: http://www.thedoorway.ca/history.php

13   For research on the U.S. self-determination projects, see articles on the Center for Self Determination website – www.centerforself-determination.com (The Center for Self-Determination is the primary clearinghouse, training, and technical assistance source on self-determination in the United States and other countries. The Center is devoted to moving power and authority over resources directly to individuals with disabilities, families and allies.)

14   Tom Chau, *Journal of Neural Engineering,* February 2009.

15   Daniel Pink, *Drive: The Surprising Truth About What Motivates Us*. New York: Riverhead books, 2009.

16   For a legal capacity definition, see http://legaldictionary.thefreedictionary.com/capacity

17   Michael Kennedy, Research and Training Center on Community Integration, Center on Human Policy, Division of Special Education and Rehabilitation, School of Education, Syracuse University, 1996.

18   For a detailed history of the Independent Living movement in Canada, see John Lord, *Impact: Changing the Way We View Disability,* Ottawa: Independent Living Canada, 2010. Also see the website of Independent Living Canada, www.ilcanada.ca

19   For a summary of key principles of recovery, see William Anthony and Kevin Ann Huckshorn, *Principled Leadership in Mental Health Systems and Programs.* Boston: Center for Psychiatric Rehabilitation, Boston University, 2008. Also see Geoffrey Nelson, John Lord, and Joanna Ochocka, *Shifting the Paradigm in Community Mental Health: Toward Empowerment and Community.* Toronto: University of Toronto Press, 2001.

20   To access resources, developed by People First of Canada, see www.peoplefirstofcanada.ca

21   To better understand how poverty-reduction initiatives are working across Canada, look at the Vital Communities projects. See www.tamarackcommunity.ca

22   National Committee for the Prevention of Elder Abuse, Autonomy and Self-determination — www.preventelderabuse.org/issues/autonomy.html

23   See John Lord and Peggy Hutchison, *Pathways to Inclusion: Building a New Story with People and Communities.* Concord, ON: Captus Press, Second Edition, 2011.

24   See Bruce Anderson, *The Teacher's Gift.* Vashon, WA: Island Press, 2006. Bruce Anderson is also part of a group called The Activators. This is a website of interest to facilitators: www.communityactivators.com

25   For a review of empowerment research, see John Lord and Peggy Hutchison, The Process of Empowerment: Implications for Theory and Practice, *Canadian Journal of Community Mental Health,* 12, 1 (1993), pp. 5-22. For reflective insights on power and control, see James Hillman, *Kinds of Power: A Guide to its Intelligent Uses.* New York: Currency Doubleday, 1995.

26   Stephen Cassetari, *Reflections on the River.* Sydney, Australia: Angus and Robertson, 1993.

27   Dalai Lama, *Shambhala Sun Magazine,* May 2009, page 13.

28   Malcolm Gladwell has written an insightful essay about the limits of generalization. See "The New-Boy Network", which appears in Malcolm Gladwell, *What the Dog Saw.* New York: Little Bay Books, 2009.

29   Robert Putnam, interview from Atlantic Unbound, *Lonely in America,* September 21, 2000.

30   See Malcolm Gladwell, *Outliers: The Story of Success*. New York: Little, Brown and Company, 2008.

31   See R. Larson, Thirty years of Research on the Subjective Well-being of Older Americans, *The Gerontological Society of America*, 33: 1, pages 109-125, 1978.

32   In 1999, the Federal government of Canada commissioned a series of studies and articles on the determinants of health. This project resulted in a five-volume series that captures the power and importance of using the determinants of health as one way to create healthy citizens. See *Canada Health Action: Building on the Legacy*, Five Volumes. Ottawa: MutiMondes and Public Works, Government Services Canada, 2000. Also see Juha Mikkonen and Dennis Raphael, *Social Determinants of Health: The Canadian Facts*. Toronto: York University School of Health Policy and Management, 2010.

33   See Juha Mikkonen and Dennis Raphael, *Social Determinants of Health: The Canadian Facts*. Toronto: York University School of Health Policy and Management, 2010.

34   See, for example, Charlotte Dingwall, *Kirby's Lane: A Well Travelled Path*. Toronto: Community Living Ontario, 2009. Also see Barbara Leavitt, Chris Hicks, Diane Peacock, *Her Shoes are Brown*. Community Involvement Council, 1993.

35   In his book on community, Al Condeluci lists several definitions of community by leading scholars. See Al Condeluci, *Interdependence: The Route to Community*. Winter Park, FL: PMD Publishers, 1991.

36   See John McKnight and Peter Block, *The Abundant Community: Awakening the Power of Families and Neighbourhoods*. San Francisco: Barrett-Koehler Publishers, 2010.

37   See Ray Oldenburg, *Celebrating the Third Place: Inspiring Stories about the "Great Good Places" at the Heart of our Communities*. New York: Marlowe and Company, 2000.

38   Sherri Torgman, *Shared Space: The Communities Agenda*. Ottawa: The Caledon Institute, 2007.

39   See Malcolm Gladwell, *Outliers: The Story of Success*. New York: Little, Brown, and Company, 2008

40   Judith Snow, personal conversation.

41   David Schultz, *Who Cares: Re-Discovering Community*. Boulder, CO: Westview, 1997.

42   Judith Snow, *Thoughts on Self Determination*. Toronto, Unpublished, March 2001.

43   See research on determinants of health, and especially Juha Mikkonen and Dennis Raphael, *The Canadian Facts: Social Determinants of Health*. Toronto: York University School of Health Policy and Management, 2010.

44   See, especially, Nicholas Christakis and James Fowler, *Connected: The Surprising*

Power of Our Social Networks and How They Shape Our Lives. New York: Little, Brown and Company, 2009.

45   Speech by Pat Worth to People First Conference in Thunder Bay, ON, 1999

46   William Paul Young quotes Sarayu in *The Shack*, pg 198, 2007.

47   Margaret Wheatley and Deborah Frieze, *Lifecycle of Emergence: Using Emergence to Take Social Innovations to Scale*, Berkana Institute, p. 1, 2006. See www.berkana.org

48   See Peggy Hutchison, John Lord, and Karen Lord, *Friends and Inclusion: Five Approaches to Building Relationships*. Toronto: Inclusion Press, 2010.

49   In recent years, several important documents on person-centred planning have been published. Facilitators will want to be aware of these resources and use them to assist them in deepening their craft. See John O'Brien and Connie Lyle O'Brien, *A Little Book About Person Centred Planning*. Toronto: Inclusion Press, 1998. Also, John O'Brien and Connie Lyle O'Brien, *Implementing Person Centred Planning*. Toronto: Inclusion Press, and John O'Brien and Carol Blessing, *Conversations on Citizenship and Person-Centred Work*, Toronto: Inclusion Press, 2011. Also John O'Brien, Jack Pearpoint, and Lynda Kahn, *The PATH and MAPS Handbook*. Toronto: Inclusion Press, 2010.

50   See, for example, John Lord and Peggy Hutchison, Individualized Funding in Ontario: Report of a Provincial Study, *Journal on Developmental Disabilities*, 14, 2, pp. 44-53, 2008. Also see Steve Holburn and Peter Vietze, *Person-Centred Planning: Research, Practice, and Future Directions*. Baltimore, MD: Paul H. Brookes Publishing, 2002

51   See Mark Raggin, *The Recovery Model*, http://www.ibhp.org/uploads/file/Recovery%20 model%20paper-Ragins.pdf

52   John Lord and Peggy Hutchison, *Pathways to Inclusion: Building a New Story with People and Communities*. Concord, ON: Captus Press, Second Edition, 2011.

53   In Ontario, for example, the *2008 Social Inclusion Act* earmarks person-directed planning as an important funded service in developmental disabilities. See www.laws.gov.on.ca/html/ statutes/english/elaws_statutes_08s14_e.htm

54   Charlotte Dingwall, Kristi Kemp, and Barb Fowke, *Creating a Good Life in Community: A Guide on Person-Directed Planning*. Toronto: Ministry of Community and Social Services, 2006.

55   This list of planning guidelines is adapted from a few key documents, including the Choices Project in Thunder Bay, the Modeling Community Change and Innovation Project, and the Individualized Funding Coalition for Ontario.

56   See Daniel Pink's book for a full analysis on the role of motivation in creating change. Pink shows how goals developed 'for' people are seldom adhered to or fully

implemented. See Daniel Pink, *Drive: The Surprising Truth About What Motivates Us*. New York: Riverhead Books, 2009.

57   Juha Mikkonen and Dennis Raphael, *The Canadian Facts: Social Determinants of Health*. Toronto: York University School of Health Policy and Management, 2010.

58   Craig Shields, *Protecting Vulnerable Adults: Lessons from the Past, Recommendations for the Future*. Toronto: Human Services Consultants, 2008.

59   Conversation with Orville Endicott, Lawyer, Community Living Ontario.

60   Louise A. Stratford, *Protecting Vulnerable Adults – A Community Responsibility Public Guardian and Trustee*; The Chief Justice of Ontario's Advisory Committee on Professionalism; The Eleventh Colloquium on the Legal Profession, 2008.

61   Simon Duffy & John Gillespie, *Personalisation & Safeguarding,* Version 1.1 (2009) This discussion paper has been written in response to the British government's review of the current *No Secrets* regulations published as *Safeguarding Adults*. It is a Version 1.1 document which means that In Control, working with its membership, will continue to improve this discussion paper as further evidence emerges.

62   *Responding To Vulnerability: A Discussion Paper About Safeguards & People With Developmental Disabilities*, 2007. Developed by Community Living British Columbia (CLBC) for Discussion with Self-advocates, Families, Service Providers, Caregivers and other Concerned People.

63   Gail Jones, *Vulnerable Adults: What are the Safety Checks*. Safeguards for Vulnerable Adults in Ontario Discussion Paper, 2007.

64   Al Etmanski, *Safe and Secure: Six steps to Creating a Good Life for People with Disabilities*. Vancouver: PLAN, Pg 173, 2010.

65   See Daniel Pink, *Drive: The Truth About What Motivates Us*. New York: Riverhead Books, 2009.

Resources for Your Review

- **Facilitation for Inclusion with PATH & MAPS** - Training DVD - J. Pearpoint & L. Kahn
- **Conversations on Citizenship & Person-Centered Planning** - John O'Brien & Carol Blessing - New
- **Flourish: People with Disabilties Living Life with Passion - Karin Melberg Schwier** - New
- **Navigating College A Handbook on Self Advocacy Written for Autistic Students from Autistic Adults** - New
- **Intentional Teaming: Shifting Organizational Culture** - Beth Gallagher & Kirk Hinkleman - New
- **Who's Drawing the Lines?** - Judith Snow - New
- **Facilitating an Everyday Life** - J. Lord, C. Dingwall, B. Leavitt - New
- **Friends & Inclusion**: Five Approaches to Building Relationships: P. Hutchison; J. Lord, K. Lord - New
- **Facilitating an Everyday Life** - J. Lord, C. Dingwall, B. Leavitt - New
- **Equity, Social Justice and Disability in Schools** - Gary Bunch et al - New
- **Facilitation for Inclusion with PATH & MAPS** - training DVD
- **PATH & MAPS Handbook:** Person-Centered Ways to Build Community - New
- **PlayFair Teams** - 2 books, DVD + Posters - blended teams in schools.
- Partnering for Children with Disabilities: A Dance that Matters - J. Fialka, A Feldman, K Mikus
- Gentle Heart Fearless Mind: Mindfulness DVD + Booklet: Alan Sloan
- Make a Difference Pack: Leader's Manual + MAD Guidebook +10 Learning Journey Booklets
- Golden Reflections: - written by Vargus Yale (Mike's seeing-eye guide dog) with Mike Yale
- Inclusive Education: Emergent Solutions   Gary Bunch & Angela Valeo
- Planning for a Real Life After School: Transition from School (2 editions)
- The Poetry of David Moreau: If You're Happy and You Know It Clap Your Hand
- Doing Our Best Work: 10 Ingredients of Quality Support: Peter Leidy - DVD
- ABCD in Action - DVD & Book -When People Care Enough to Act
- My Life My Choice - DVD - Seven Adults living full lives in the community
- Make a Difference - book; Leaders Guide, Work Booklets
- The Big Plan - A Good Life After School - Transition Planning with groups
- Each Belongs - book & CD - The 1st Inclusive School Board ever!
- Find Meaning in the Work - CD & Manual/Curriculum - presentation ready!
- Free to Fly - A Story of Manic Depression - Caroline Fei-Yeng Kwok

Download
our Catalogue:
http://inclusion.com

INCLUSION PRESS

47 Indian Trail, Toronto,
Ontario Canada M6R 1Z8
p. 416.658.5363 f. 416.658.5067
e. inclusionpress@inclusion.com

inclusion.com   BOOKS • WORKSHOPS • MEDIA • RESOURCES

The Power of Three - Mobilizing Gifts and Capacity

Skillful facilitators know that person centered planning and community engagement involves more than technique:
- it's a form of relationship;
- a commitment to a well-developed set of values and practices;
- a way of thinking and engagement.

These three books are powerful approaches for:
- finding, organizing and mobilizing community capacity (ABCD);
- for discovering gifts and capacities in everyone to make a difference by
- building relationships that support people to be contributing citizens (MAD);
- deepening practices of Facilitation, exploring the powers of facilitators,
- practicing the conditions for success in convening conversations.

They offer powerful questions for the conversational patterns of PATH and MAPS to take good intentions into action (PATH & MAPS Handbook).

A powerful combination pack of practices and learning.

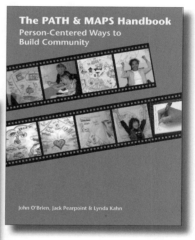

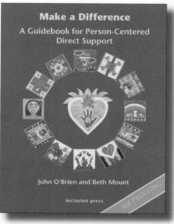

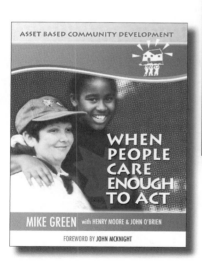

Writings that lay foundations for discovering and mobilizing the gifts and capacities of people and communities.

**Power of Three Pack
(all three books)**
$70.00 plus shipping & taxes as applicable

INCLUSION PRESS

47 Indian Trail, Toronto
Ontario Canada M6R 1Z8
p. 416.658.5363
f. 416.658.5067
inclusionpress@inclusion.com

inclusion.com   BOOKS ·WORKSHOPS · MEDIA

Conversations on
Citizenship &
Person-Centered Work
Edited by John O'Brien & Carol Blessing

Beth Mount

Michael Smull

Denise Bissonnette

Diana Whitney

Jack Pearpoint

Connie Ferrell

Mike Green

Carol Blessing

John O'Brien

Meet developers of…

…approaches to person-centered work:

Personal Futures Planning • MAPS • PATH • Person-Centered Thinking Tools
Essential Lifestyle Planning • Cultivating True Livelihood • Framework for Planning

…approaches to organizational & community development:

Appreciative Inquiry • Asset Based Community Development: ABCD

in conversation with Carol Blessing about citizenship, community, disability, employment & social change in response to questions like these:

What does it take to make connections between people with disabilities and community associations?

What drew you to your work?

What keeps people with disabilities from full citizenship?

What are the principles of effective supported employment?

What do we have to give up in order to move to person-centered work?

How do you judge the effectiveness of person-centered work?

How does ABCD compliment person-centered practices?

What are the risks of person-centered planning?

Are there times when person-centered planning does not work?

How do person-centered thinking skills contribute to change in organizations and systems?

How do you respond to people who say that implementing person-centered work is too costly?

What is citizenship?

What is leadership?

What inspires you?

What is community?

What does it take to sustain us in this work?

Why is courage important in person-centered work?

What are the core principles of Appreciative Inquiry?

What strategies implement Appreciative Leadership?

> **Conversations:**
> $25.00 plus shipping & handling

This book was developed to support the Cornell University Citizen-Centered Leadership Community of Practice.
www.citizencenteredleadership.com

INCLUSION PRESS

47 Indian Trail, Toronto
Ontario Canada M6R 1Z8
p. 416.658.5363 f. 416.658.5067
inclusionpress@inclusion.com

inclusion.com

BOOKS • WORKSHOPS • MEDIA